"Larry Osborne combines winsome humor, brutal honesty, and keen insights about mistakes that good-hearted leaders are making. Read this book."
— *Matt Chandler, author,* The Explicit Gospel

"Larry Osborne has written many great books, but this is his best. As I read each chapter, I kept thinking how desperately the church needs to hear this message. Every believer should read it."
— *Rick Warren, author,* The Purpose Driven Life

"It is tempting to see Pharisees everywhere but in our own hearts. This book gives us pause to examine our motives, movements, and ministries in light of Scripture and to live out the gospel in fresh and freeing ways."
— *Ed Stetzer, President, LifeWay Research*

"I am part of one of the movements Larry critiques. I found his insights not only helpful but prophetic. Thank you, Larry, for helping me understand the Bible, contemporary movements, and my own heart better."
— *JD Greear, Pastor, Summit Church*

"I was thankful Larry Osborne wrote this book for some Pharisees I know. After reading it, I was convicted that he wrote it for me."
— *Gene Appel, Senior Pastor, Eastside Christian Church*

"This is a book you start reading so you can recommend it to those who really need it, and around the third page, you realize it's for you."
— *Pete Briscoe, Pastor, Bent Tree Bible Fellowship*

"Larry Osborne has written a brilliant and timely corrective for the body of Christ. I laughed and cried as I recognized myself and others in this book."
— *Ray Bentley, Maranatha Chapel*

"Once again, Larry Osborne has found a way to question the unquestionable assumptions of our day and move us toward a greater understanding of Scripture. Larry helps us balance a pure devotion to God with a compassionate grace toward lost and broken people."
— *Scott Chapman, Senior Pastor, The Chapel*

"This book helped me to be a better follower of Christ. I came away challenged, sharpened, and stirred."
— *Wayne Cordeiro, author,* Jesus: Pure and Simple

"With lots of leaders bent on raising the spiritual-formation bar higher and higher, Larry brings an important word of caution. It is a word we all need to hear." — *Chris Dolson, Blackhawk Church*

"Religion is ridiculous. It causes Christians to be more 'holy' than Christ. If you want to keep taking Jesus seriously but stop taking yourself too seriously, this book is for you." —*Mark Driscoll, Mars Hill Church*

"Larry's advocacy for a more nuanced understanding of discipleship is at once both alarming and refreshing: alarming in how easy it is to become an accidental Pharisee, refreshing in opening the doors of discipleship for everyone." — *Tom Hughes, Pastor, Eagle Rock*

"Larry takes us straight to the central truths of Christianity. Every Christian should read this book. I know I need it on my bookshelf, and I need to read it regularly."
—*Shawn Lovejoy, author,* The Measure of Our Success: An Impassioned Plea to Pastors

"This book tackles one of the great tensions in the Christian life, the tension between perfection and grace. You will be challenged, comforted, and encouraged."
—*Mel Ming, Executive Director, Northwest Ministry Network, Assemblies of God*

"I am so glad Larry wrote this book, because it outlines a dangerous journey that every Christian can plunge into if we're not careful. This book will help anyone who has accidentally gone down that road to get back on the right path." — *Perry Nobel, Pastor, New Spring Church*

"Larry Osborne has written his most important book yet. This is a must-read for pastors and leaders. Reading it is like taking medicine to cure an infection." — *Rick Olmstead, Vineyard USA National Leadership Team*

"This is a truly amazing book. Such wisdom is hard to find. If you don't like it, something is seriously wrong with you. You need to get right with God." — *Carolyn Osborne, Larry's Mom*

"Jesus reserved his harshest words for the religious people of his day. The truth is, there's a little bit of religion in all of us, and a lot of it in the church. This book is a needed resource for recovering Pharisees like us." —*Darrin Patrick, Lead Pastor, The Journey*

"This is Larry Osborne's best work yet. It will convict and encourage you. We're all guilty of being accidental Pharisees from time to time. Read this book to understand how and why it happens to well-meaning Christians."
— *Linda Stanley, Leadership Network*

"Accidental Pharisee? What an extraordinary thought! Larry Osborne has touched a nerve with these life-changing words."
— *Dino Rizzo, Lead Pastor, Healing Place Church*

"Over the years, and always at just the right time, God has used Larry Osborne to speak into my life. With *Accidental Pharisees*, Larry has struck another nerve."
— *Nelson Searcy, Lead Pastor, The Journey Church*

"This book is a much-needed message for the body of Christ. A must-read for those who feel called to leadership in the local church."
— *Toby Slough, Pastor, Cross Timbers Community Church*

"Can pride be worse than porn? Larry Osborne shows us the danger of becoming poor, blind, and naked without even knowing it, and of accidentally becoming what we disdain."
— *Stacy Spencer, Pastor, New Direction Christian Church*

"I hated this book because I recognized myself in several chapters. I also loved it because it is a fresh and much-needed corrective to our excesses and oftentimes to our lack of humility."
— *Steve Stroope, author,* Tribal Church

"This book is for all of us seeking to follow Jesus fully and completely without falling into the sins of pride and arrogance."
— *Dave Travis, CEO, Leadership Network*

"Mixing humor with biblical wisdom, Larry's words are like a surgeon's scalpel—they cut you where you need it."
— *Ken Werlein, Founding Pastor, Faithbridge Church*

"Destined to be a classic. The breakthrough ideas in this biblically solid book are especially relevant for the 'company of the committed.' I am going to buy a box for those I have equipped to start churches and ministries."
— *John Worcester, Church Planting Specialist*

"A friend is someone who tells you when you have broccoli stuck between your teeth before you spend the evening smiling and making a fool of yourself. In *Accidental Pharisees*, Larry Osborne is that friend."
— *Ron Forseth, Vice President, Outreach, Inc.*

"With his probing but gracious style, Osborne confronts an important issue in the church today. He's challenging and provocative, but always biblical. He offers a needed caution and corrective for all who desire to contend for the faith."   —*William J. Hamel, President, EFCA*

"Larry Osborne has a knack for communicating pointed truths with a fatherly tenderness. As I flipped open the pages of this book, I was prepared to point my mental finger at all the religious hypocrites in our world. Instead, I was struck with two paradoxical truths: I am a Pharisee, and God loves me anyway."   —*Noel Heikkinen, Pastor, Riverview Church*

"This is a much-needed word for the church today. Larry reminds us that God's kingdom is bigger than ours. This book should be mandatory reading for every pastor."   —*Chip Henderson, Pastor, Pinelake Church*

"Larry Osborne has tackled one of the most challenging issues facing the kingdom of God. This book will enlighten and strengthen anyone who is serious about providing genuine leadership to our society."
—*John Jenkins, Pastor, First Baptist Church of Glenarden*

"Larry Osborne nails one of the main culprits eroding the advancement of the gospel: we have accidentally become Pharisees. This is one of the most important books of our generation."   —*Tyler Jones, Pastor, Vintage 21*

"Larry Osborne is one of the important sages in the American church. With candor and wisdom, he points out that the difference between a fervent disciple and a legalistic Pharisee is often not as great as we might think."   —*Geoff Surratt, Exponential Network*

"Larry Osborne takes a refreshing look at an old problem in today's church. A painfully insightful but much-needed book for all of us."
—*Ron Sylvia, Lead Pastor, Church @ The Springs*

"I have been waiting for this book for forty years. Larry Osborne warns us and helps us to protect ourselves from the ancient but living trap of religious pride and its cluster of hidden but destructive cohorts."
—*Mark Foreman, Lead Pastor, North Coast Calvary Chapel*

ACCIDENTAL
PHARISEES

Other Books by Larry Osborne

*A Contrarian's Guide to Knowing God:
Spirituality for the Rest of Us*

*Measuring Up: The Need to Succeed
and the Fear of Failure*
(with Stuart Briscoe and Knute Larson)

Sticky Church

*Sticky Teams: Keeping Your Leadership
Team and Staff on the Same Page*

*The Unity Factor: Developing
a Healthy Church Leadership Team*

LARRY OSBORNE

ACCIDENTAL
PHARISEES

AVOIDING PRIDE,
EXCLUSIVITY,
AND THE
OTHER DANGERS
OF OVERZEALOUS
FAITH

ZONDERVAN®

ZONDERVAN.com/
AUTHORTRACKER
follow your favorite authors

ZONDERVAN

Accidental Pharisees
Copyright © 2012 by Larry Osborne

This title is also available as a Zondervan ebook.
Visit www.zondervan.com/ebooks.

Requests for information should be addressed to:

Zondervan, *Grand Rapids, Michigan 49530*

Library of Congress Cataloging-in-Publication Data

Osborne, Larry W., 1952–
    Accidental pharisees : avoiding pride, exclusivity, and the other dangers of
overzealous faith / Larry Osborne.
        p. cm.
    ISBN 978-0-310-49444-7 (softcover)
    1. Christian life. 2. Pharisees. I. Title.
BV4501.3.O825 2012
    248.4—dc23   2012019463

Cover design: Ann Gjeldum / Cadmium Design
Interior design: Matthew Van Zomeren

Printed in the United States of America

12 13 14 15 16 17 18 /DCI/ 20 19 18 17 16 15 14 13 12 11 10 9 8 7 6 5 4 3 2 1

To Bill and Carolyn Osborne,
who showed me what it means
to follow Jesus without being a Pharisee

and to Wally Norling,
a mentor who taught me how to believe
in young guys by believing in me
when few others did

CONTENTS

Part 3
EXCLUSIVITY
When Thinning the Herd Becomes More Important Than Expanding the Kingdom

Part 4
LEGALISM
When Sacrifice Crowds Out Mercy

Part 5
IDOLIZING THE PAST
When Idealism Distorts Reality

Part 6
THE QUEST FOR UNIFORMITY
How Uniformity Destroys Unity

Part 7
GIFT PROJECTION
When My Calling Becomes Everyone Else's Calling

PART 1

ACCIDENTAL PHARISEES

The Dark and Dangerous Side
of Overzealous Faith

CHAPTER 1

ACCIDENTAL PHARISEES

The Dark and Dangerous Side of Overzealous Faith

Let's be honest.

Passionate faith can have a dark side — a really dark side.

Just ask Jesus.

When he showed up as God in the flesh, those who thought of themselves as God's biggest fans and defenders wanted nothing to do with him. They tried to shut him up. When they couldn't, they had him killed.

That's obviously passion gone bad.

But the ancient Pharisees aren't the only example of the dark side of overzealous faith. Our history books are filled with other examples. Think of the Crusades or the Inquisition, for starters.

But that's not why I've written this book. It's not about ancient Pharisees. It's about *accidental Pharisees* — people like you and me who, despite the best of intentions and a desire to honor God, unwittingly end up pursuing an overzealous model of faith that sabotages the work of the Lord we think we're serving.

The problem is not spiritual zeal. That's a good thing. We're all called to be zealous for the Lord.[1] The problem is unaligned spiritual passion, a zeal for the Lord that fails to line up with the totality of Scripture.

UNALIGNED ZEAL

Unfortunately, most of us think of unaligned zeal as someone else's problem. We have a hard time seeing it in ourselves.

It's easy to see the scriptural misalignment in the crazy guy on the street corner with the "Turn or Burn" sign. The same with the cut-and-paste theology of people who toss out the Scriptures they don't like. It's also easy to spot it in the pompous coworker with a big Bible on his desk, a chip on his shoulder, and a tiny heart in his chest—the self-proclaimed great witness for the Lord—whom everyone tries to avoid and no one wants to eat lunch with.

But we seldom see it in the mirror.

That's because for most of us, areas of biblically unaligned and overzealous faith are unintentional. They're the result of blind spots, not sin spots. We're doing our best with the knowledge we have.

But it doesn't matter whether someone is overzealous by choice or by accident. Either way, it messes up everything. It hurts everyone, the overzealous and the victims of their zeal.

JERKS FOR JESUS

You've probably known a jerk for Jesus, someone who thought they were advancing the cause of the kingdom when in reality they were simply embarrassing the King.

I think of a man in our church who sees himself as a mature, front-of-the-line Christian. He's passionate about the Scriptures. Loves to study. Digs deep. He knows far more than most, so he's taken it upon himself to become a spiritual watchdog to protect the rest of us.

He barks at and then attacks anyone who misspeaks or who

---

1. Rom. 12:11.

misuses or misunderstands the Bible. He thinks he's helping out Jesus by keeping the heretics out.

But all he does is scare the hell out of people.

Not literally. Just figuratively, unfortunately.

The problem is that God never asked him to be a pit bull for right doctrine. God does ask him (and all of us) to contend for the faith. But he asks us to do it in a manner exactly opposite of the way my pit bull friend defends the gospel. We're supposed to avoid quarreling, to be kind, and to gently instruct people who oppose us.[2]

My friend's pit bull methodology illustrates the biggest problem with overzealous faith and the reason why it's so hard to self-diagnose. It's almost always true to Scripture, but it's not true to *all* of Scripture. It's partially right. It fixates on one area of God's will (for instance, defending the faith) while ignoring other parts (doing so kindly and gently).

Unfortunately, for most of us, when we think of having overzealous faith and being a jerk for Jesus, we picture someone with bad breath, bad theology, and no people skills. So it never dawns on us that we could be included.

But the fact is, we all have areas of unaligned faith and incomplete understanding. We all have blind spots, and we all have sin spots; when the two mix, it's a dangerous combination. It's hard to get everything right. That's why I call those of us who step over the line into overzealous and unaligned faith accidental Pharisees. We've stumbled into a place we never wanted to go.

ACCIDENTAL PHARISEES

No one starts out with the desire to become a Pharisee. They're the bad guys. We all know that. In the same way, no one ever looks in the mirror and sees a Pharisee. I've never heard anyone describe himself as a Pharisee. I bet you haven't either. The word always describes someone else.

But the truth is that accidental Pharisees are made up of people just like you and me, people who love God, love the Scriptures,

---

2. Jude 3–4; 2 Tim. 2:24–26.

and are trying their best to live by them. The thing to note about accidental Pharisees is just that. They're accidental. They're like dinner at Denny's. No one plans to go there. You just end up there.

So how does it happen? What are the early warning signs? What do we need to watch out for?

THE INNOCENT AND DANGEROUS PATH

The journey to becoming an accidental Pharisee usually starts out innocently enough. It's often triggered by an eye-opening event.

Sometimes it's a mission trip, a conference, or a powerful new book. Sometimes it's a small group experience that makes everything else feel like you've just been playing church. Or perhaps it's a new Bible teacher who opens your eyes to things you've never seen before.

So you step out in faith. You make some big changes. You clean up areas of sin and compromise. You add new spiritual disciplines as you excitedly race off toward the front of the following-Jesus line.

But as you press forward, it's inevitable that you begin to notice that some people lag behind. And it's at this point that your personal pursuit of holiness can morph into something dangerous: a deepening sense of frustration with those who don't share your passionate pursuit of holiness.

This is the critical juncture.

If you allow your frustration to turn into disgust and disdain for people you've left behind, you'll end up on a dangerous detour. Instead of becoming more like Jesus, you'll become more like his archenemies, the Pharisees of old, looking down on others, confident in your own righteousness.

That, of course, is a terrible place to be.

But actually it can get worse.

If you continue farther down the path of contempt for those who fail to keep up, you'll end up in a place of arrogance. Fewer and fewer people will measure up to your definition of a genuine disciple. Inevitably, being right will become more important than being kind, gracious, or loving. Thinning the herd will become more important than expanding the kingdom. Unity will take a back seat to uniformity.[3]

And your metamorphosis will be complete. You will have arrived at a place you never intended to go. You'll be a full-fledged Pharisee. Accidental, no doubt. But a Pharisee nonetheless.

In the following pages, we'll discover how to recognize and avoid these dangers. We'll turn to the words of Jesus to uncover the early warning signs of a budding Pharisee and to expose the subtle indicators that a particular path of discipleship (even if well worn and hugely popular) is actually a spiritually treacherous detour to avoid.

In addition, if you're a parent or serve in a position of spiritual leadership, we'll look at steps you can take to make sure that the things you teach, the structures you create, and the way you lead don't unintentionally foster the dark and dangerous side of overzealous faith — or worse yet, create your own little brood of accidental Pharisees.

But first, we need to begin with an accurate understanding of what it means to be a Pharisee. Who were the Pharisees? How did their name become associated with hypocrisy and misguided zeal for God? And exactly how short (and subtle) is the journey from high commitment to high treason?

---

3. Eph. 4:1–6; 1 Cor. 13:1–7.

CHAPTER 2

THE "P" WORD

How Did the Pharisees Get Such a Bad Rap?

A few years ago I had the opportunity to speak at a friend's church. I started by telling everyone how happy I was to be there. I then shared how their pastor had told me that his church was full of Pharisees. I told them that after spending a few days with the staff and key leaders, I had to agree. They were quite possibly the most pharisaical church I'd ever been to.

The room got strangely quiet — that awkward silence that comes when you don't know whether to be angry with the idiot who just said something offensive or to feel sorry for the poor slob.

I stopped and asked if something was wrong.

The room grew even quieter.

Finally, there were a couple of stifled laughs. Then a few knowing nods. Eventually the rest of the room got it. I hadn't misspoken. I was simply having some fun at their expense. I was messing with them.

So I asked another question. "How many of you considered my introduction to be an insult instead of a compliment?"

Nearly every hand was raised.

I went on to explain that calling someone a Pharisee wasn't always considered such a social faux pas. In fact, in Jesus' day it would have been a great way to start a sermon. I was just a couple of thousand years too late.

Today, when most of us hear the word *Pharisee*, we conjure up images of hypocritical, narrow-minded, puffed-up spiritual losers. But in Jesus' day, being called a Pharisee was a badge of honor. It was a compliment, not a slam.

That's because first-century Pharisees excelled in everything we admire spiritually. They were zealous for God, completely committed to their faith. They were theologically astute, masters of the biblical texts. They fastidiously obeyed even the most obscure commands. They even made up extra rules just in case they were missing anything. Their embrace of spiritual disciplines was second to none.

Yes, they could be a bit harsh and arrogant at times. But most of their contemporaries took it in stride. After all, the Pharisees had earned the right to boast and look down on everyone else. They were paying a price no one else was willing to pay.

The Pharisees were held in such high regard that both Jesus and the apostle Paul played the Pharisee card when they wanted to illustrate the highest levels of spiritual commitment. They knew their audience would be impressed.

THE DAY JESUS PLAYED THE PHARISEE CARD

Jesus first played the Pharisee card in his famous Sermon on the Mount. To illustrate the impossibility of earning our way into heaven, he pointed to a series of well-known moral standards from the law of Moses, then added to each one a much higher standard—one that was impossible to reach.

Using the words "You have heard ..., but I tell you ...," he took six commands they thought they could keep and replaced each one with a standard they could never achieve.

Don't commit murder became don't even be angry with your brother, and don't label him an idiot or call him a fool no matter what he's done.

Don't commit adultery turned into a prohibition of lustful

thoughts and wandering eyes. There was an additional instruction for people who had a hard time achieving victory in this area: they were to gouge out their eye and cut off their hand if they wanted to see the kingdom of heaven.

Now, *that* had to freak out his listeners.

Shoot, it freaks me out.

It's one thing to forbid adultery. It's another to classify a lustful look as adultery in my heart. But it's downright terrifying to think that we have to gouge out our eye or cut off our hand if we struggle with taking a second look.

Obviously, Jesus wasn't asking people to literally pluck out an eye or cut off a hand. He was simply driving home his point: We can't earn our way into God's favor by meticulously following a moral code—even a biblical one. Our deeds will never be righteous enough. God's standard of holiness is way beyond our best efforts.

But just to make sure that everyone understood how impossible it is to stand before God justified by our own good deeds and righteousness, Jesus bookended his six shocking and impossible-to-keep standards with two stunning statements:

1. He started out by saying, *"Unless your righteousness surpasses that of the Pharisees* and the teachers of the law, you will certainly not enter the kingdom of heaven."[1]
2. He ended by saying, "Be perfect, therefore, as your heavenly Father is perfect."[2]

Those two statements had to be incredibly disturbing to his listeners. There was no way they could be as perfect as their heavenly Father. And since the Pharisees were considered to be the most righteous of the righteous, surpassing them was also out of the question.

They were doomed!

I guarantee you, no one who heard Jesus that day thought, "I can't be as perfect as the heavenly Father, but at least I can surpass

---

1. Matt. 5:20, emphasis added.
2. Matt. 5:48.

the righteousness of the Pharisees. Those guys are a bunch of self-righteous losers."

No. They were stunned. They had to be thinking, "That's impossible!" Which was exactly what Jesus wanted them to think. His goal was to point them to the cross. He wanted them to understand that they couldn't pull off their own salvation. He'd have to do it for them.

And that's why he played the Pharisee card. He knew they'd be blown away that the people they thought were closest to God weren't close enough.

PAUL'S PHARISEE CARD

But Jesus wasn't the only one to play the Pharisee card. So did the apostle Paul. He used the people's high regard for the Pharisees to illustrate the absolute supremacy and sufficiency of Jesus Christ.

To do so, Paul reached back into his past. He pulled out his résumé to point out that he had once been a card-carrying Pharisee in good standing. Then he proceeded to trash the benefits of being a Pharisee in good standing by claiming that they were worthless rubbish in comparison with being found in Christ.

Actually, he used a much stronger word than *rubbish*. My editor won't let me put it in writing. So you'll have to look up the meaning of the word for yourself. But I warn you. If you say it, your mother might wash your mouth out with soap.[3]

Paul's words must have shocked his readers. Not for their earthiness but for his total disregard of *any* of the spiritual benefits that came with being a Pharisee. Pharisees were considered the most committed of the committed. Their passion, discipline, and biblical commitment were exemplary. It was hard to imagine that it could all be worthless. Which is exactly why Paul played his Pharisee card.

He knew that his rejection of all the things he accomplished as a Pharisee would powerfully drive home his point: that Jesus, the

---

3. Phil. 3:3–12. The Greek word translated as *garbage* or *rubbish* is *skubala*, which literally means "excrement," nicely translated as *dung* in some translations.

cross, and the resurrection are far better than anything we could ever achieve on our own.

WHY THIS IS SO IMPORTANT

These insights into the high regard that the contemporaries of Jesus and Paul had for the Pharisees are more than mere tidbits of ancient history. They are important for every Christian to grasp, for one simple reason. If we fail to understand how spiritually impressive the Pharisees were, we will remain blind to the danger of becoming like them. We'll assume that their tragic transformation from passionate defenders of God into mortal enemies of God could never happen to us.

Don't forget, the Pharisees of old saw themselves as God's biggest fans. They praised him. They worshiped him. They spoke out in his defense. Yet when he showed up, they vehemently opposed him.

In the same way, we can wax eloquent about Jesus and the Scriptures. We can praise him. Sing to him. Speak out in his defense. Yet when he shows up in ways that we don't expect, that we don't agree with, or that make us uncomfortable, we can fight him tooth and nail.

The bottom line is that as long as my only image of a Pharisee is that of a spiritual loser and a perennial enemy of Jesus, I'll never recognize the clear and present danger in my own life. I'll never realize that it's often a very short and subtle journey from being zealous for God to being unintentionally opposed to God.

THE GOOD NEWS FOR AN ACCIDENTAL PHARISEE

There is no getting around the harsh fact. Some of the Pharisees in Jesus' day earned a one-way ticket to hell. Jesus was quite clear. They thought they would hear, "Well done, good and faithful servant!" but they heard instead, "I never knew you. Away from me, you evildoers!"[4]

---

4. Matt. 25:21; 7:21–23.

Yet, thankfully, for some of the other Pharisees the outcome was different. Their detour down the path of spiritual pride, exclusivity, and the other traits of Phariseeism was a costly mistake, but it wasn't a one-way ticket to perdition. They suffered loss, to be sure. All the rewards they thought they were storing up gained them nothing.[5] But in the end, their jaunt down the Pharisee path was simply a temporary detour. Somehow their eyes were opened. They turned back.

I think of Nicodemus.[6]

I think of a Pharisee named Saul. We know him as the apostle Paul.[7]

I think of my own trek down this tempting path.

My Calvinist friends say God pulled me back. My Arminian friends say I chose to come back. We can fight that one out in another book. But either way, the important thing is that people who start down this path—and even those who go a long way down it—can still come to their senses, turn back, and head home.

There's always an off-ramp. There's always the opportunity to make a U-turn.

---

5. Matt. 6:1–18; 1 Cor. 3:12–14.
6. John 3:1–2.
7. Phil. 3:1–7.

CHAPTER 3

JOSEPH OF ARIMATHEA

The Disciple Nobody Wants to Be

Not long ago I found myself shocked by a disciple I thought I knew. His name is Joseph of Arimathea. Jesus was buried in his tomb. He makes a cameo appearance in all four gospels, then disappears.

I was well aware of his name. But I knew little about the man. I thought his role in the story of Holy Week was insignificant, a brief sidebar, unworthy of a deep dive.

I knew that he was a disciple.

I knew that he courageously stepped forward to ask for Jesus' body.

I knew Jesus was placed in Joseph's tomb.

But I had missed something incredibly important. I had never noticed what kind of disciple he was. He was the disciple none of us want to be.

If you read his story carefully, comparing all four gospel accounts, it becomes evident that if he were alive today (and if we didn't know the end of his story), most of us would write him off as a loser. He'd be the poster child for a counterfeit disciple.

He's exactly the kind of Christ follower that most speakers preach against, ridicule, and warn us not to become.

Let me explain.

WHAT JESUS REQUIRES

There's always a great deal of discussion in theological circles as to what constitutes a genuine disciple. Should the barrier to entry be low, or is it supposed to be high? Did Jesus come to let the riffraff in or to drive the lukewarm out?

The politically correct answer changes every few decades. It swings from one extreme to the other.

For a while there's a huge emphasis on evangelism. The goal is to get folks saved. The dream is to fill up heaven. There's not much attention given to discipleship. Maturity is mostly an afterthought.

That's followed by a pendulum swing toward discipleship. The goal is to bring people to maturity. The dream is a church full of on-fire disciples. There's not much patience for the struggling. Those who are fearful, hesitant, or not yet fully convinced are asked to leave.

That's the stage we're in today. Conferences, books, and keynote speakers emphasize giving it all to Jesus. Spiritual burnout is once again a badge of honor. In some circles, it's almost a contest to see who's willing to give up the most to follow Jesus.

A booklet that recently came across my desk put it this way: "Plainly put, a relationship with Jesus *requires* absolute, undivided, exclusive affection."[1]

I read that and thought, "Really?"

So there's no relationship with Jesus unless he has our absolute, undivided, exclusive affection? Absolute? Undivided? Exclusive?

If that's true, there's going to be a lot of Christians in hell. An awful lot.

I might be there.

There's no question that Jesus sets a high standard. He told a

---

1. David Platt, *The Radical Question* (Sisters, Ore.: Multnomah, 2010), 13, emphasis added.

rich young ruler to sell all he had. He told a man waiting for his father to die that waiting wasn't an option. He told his followers to expect hatred and death. He told us to pick up our cross and carry it daily.[2] But he also said and did some things that no one seems to talk about much these days.

For instance, he healed a fearful woman who tried to sneak in for a magical touch. He praised her for her faith, despite its obvious timidity.[3] He knew Peter would deny him, but he kept him around anyway. He even pursued him afterward. He gave him a pretty cool assignment too.[4] He went out of his way to show himself to a doubting Thomas. And he didn't show up to kick him off the team. He showed up to help him overcome his doubt.[5]

Even more surprising, Jesus encouraged crowds of weary and spiritually burdened people to come to him for rest, a lighter load, and an easy yoke.[6]

That's right — rest, a lighter load, and an easy yoke. Try preaching that message today. You'll be blasted as a compromiser, an advocate of comfortable consumer Christianity.

WHAT HAPPENED TO THE EPISTLES?

I've noticed something else recently. When it comes to discipleship, many Protestants have adopted a decidedly Roman Catholic approach to Scripture. Catholics stand when the Gospels are read and sit for the Epistles.

Many of today's best-known discipleship pundits do essentially the same thing. Their theology and paradigm of what it means to follow Jesus is based almost exclusively on the words of Jesus. Little attention is paid to the context of his sayings or how the New Testament epistles interpret and apply his teachings.

There is no arguing that Jesus demands and deserves our absolute allegiance. If he's God in the flesh, anything less is a

---

2. Mark 10:17–22; Luke 9:21–26, 59–62.
3. Mark 5:25–34.
4. Luke 22:31–34; John 21:1–19.
5. John 20:24–29.
6. Matt. 11:28–30.

fool's response. But it's a huge mistake to interpret his strongest and harshest statements in a vacuum. That might make for powerful sound bites, but it also makes for bad theology.

To correctly understand what Jesus wants from us, we must include *all* of his sayings and *all* of his actions. In addition, we can't leave out the writings of the apostles. After all, they were rather close to the action. Their interpretations are authoritative.

Let's look at just one example.

When Jesus says to leave everything behind, die to self, and follow him, what does it mean to us today?

For people who focus primarily on Jesus' words in red, it's a no-brainer. Jesus wants all of us to forego the comforts of home and head overseas or into the inner city. If we can't do that, we should at least take some short-term mission trips and ratchet down our lifestyle so that we can more generously support those who go.

But is that really what Jesus wants? Is that really his calling for the vast majority of us?

I think not.

And here's why.

A full and careful reading of the Gospels reveals that Jesus asked only a few specific individuals to leave everything behind and follow him. He actually told some who wanted to join him to stay behind.[7] He never asked the crowds to pack up and follow him from town to town. At the end of the day, he sent them home.

In addition, not one of the writers of the New Testament epistles exhorts his readers to head out to the mission field or to join Paul and Peter in planting churches. In fact, quite the opposite. Paul instructs the people in Corinth to bloom where they're planted, and the people in Thessalonica to live a quiet life and mind their own business.[8]

Whatever it means to take up our cross and follow Jesus, these passages have to be included in the mix. We can't take a few of

---

7. Mark 5:18–20.
8. 1 Cor. 7:17–20; 1 Thess. 4:11.

Jesus' statements and turn them into a global assignment and responsibility for all. We have to interpret his words in light of the *totality* of Scripture. Anything else is cut-and-paste theology.

WHY JOSEPH OF ARIMATHEA IS SO IMPORTANT

That's why the story of Joseph of Arimathea is so important. It's paradigm-busting. It messes with many of our preconceived notions about Jesus, discipleship, what it means to please God, and the kind of person God uses.

Let's see how.

As mentioned above, I'd always thought of Joseph as a bit player in the resurrection narratives. The key players were people directly involved in the death and resurrection. Jesus' burial was simply the connecting point between the two. Joseph and his tomb were necessary, but in the same way that a conjunction is needed in a longer sentence.

That's because I assumed that dead bodies are always buried somewhere. But nothing could be farther from the truth. In the first century, the body of a condemned criminal was dumped on the rubbish heap. It was left for scavenging dogs and vultures.

No Joseph of Arimathea.

No body to resurrect.

No empty tomb to point to.

Don't miss this. Joseph was the *only* disciple who stepped forward to take the body. All the others were nowhere to be found. A few of the women hung around to see what would happen next. But everyone else apparently was so shell-shocked and heartbroken that they left.

But that's not all. Joseph's actions also fulfilled an important messianic prophecy.

Isaiah had prophesied that the Suffering Servant would die as a condemned man and be assigned to the grave of the wicked, but he would be buried with the rich.[9] That's a strange combination.

---

9. Isa. 53:9.

Yet because Joseph was a rich man, and because Jesus was buried in his tomb, the prophecy was fulfilled to the letter.

(By the way, I've often asked myself why it was important for Jesus to be buried with the rich. Perhaps it was simply to fulfill a bizarre prophecy that no one else could claim to have fulfilled. But there may be another reason as well. Perhaps his burial in a fancy tomb was the first step in his exaltation. Paul writes in Philippians that *because* Jesus humbled himself by foregoing heaven, taking on human form, and then dying on the cross, he was highly exalted. Jesus' first step of humiliation was the poverty of a borrowed manger. Perhaps his first step of exaltation was the honor of burial with the rich. Who knows? I'd like to ask him about it someday).[10]

But no matter why God chose a rich man's tomb, it was Joseph he used to pull it off. And without Joseph, Jesus' body would have been dumped on the rubbish heap to be devoured long before Easter morning.

AN UNLIKELY HERO

Not only is Joseph an unappreciated hero. He's also an unlikely hero. To see what I mean, let's start with Matthew and work our way through John.

A Rich Disciple?

The first thing we learn is that Joseph was rich. Not formerly rich but currently rich. We also discover that he'd already been a disciple for a while.[11]

So we have a rich disciple, which is already a problem for people who think that *rich* and *disciple* are two words that don't go together.

A Powerful Political Figure?

Mark adds that Joseph was also a prominent member of the Sanhedrin, a powerful group of seventy-one men who functioned

---

10. Philippians 2:8–9 says of Jesus after his humiliation, "Therefore God exalted him."

11. Matt. 27:57.

more or less as the Supreme Court of Israel. They were also the people who turned Jesus over to Pilate.[12]

So now we have a rich disciple who is a prestigious member of the group that condemned Jesus to death and turned him over to Pilate. But if you think that's confusing, it gets worse.

A Righteous Man?

Luke adds that he was a good and upright (literally righteous) man who had not consented to the Council's decision to turn Jesus over to Pilate.[13]

But that begs the question, If he was a disciple and a righteous man and didn't agree with the decision, why didn't he step forward to stop it? After all, he wasn't just a junior member of the Sanhedrin. He was a prominent member. Yet none of the gospel accounts even hint at any resistance surfacing within the Council. In fact, they imply strong consensus.

So now we have an even more confusing picture. We've got a rich disciple with a prominent position in the political body that turned Jesus over to Pilate. He's called a good and upright man, yet he seems to do nothing to stop the travesty of Jesus' trial.

But it gets even more perplexing.

A Secret Disciple?

John tells us that Joseph was a secret disciple and that he laid low because he was afraid of his fellow Jewish leaders. In other words, he feared losing his wealth and his status, so he hid in the weeds until after Jesus' death.[14]

I don't know about you, but I'd hardly call that the behavior of a righteous man or a disciple. In fact, I've always thought that "secret disciple" was an oxymoron.

Frankly, if I came across a modern-day Joseph, I'd be more likely to call him a fraud and phony than a disciple. I might even

---

12. Mark 15:42–47.
13. Luke 23:50–58.
14. John 19:38–42.

use him as an example of everything that's wrong with the shallow and uncommitted Christianity of our day.

Except for one small problem. Jesus didn't call him out, write him off, or tear him apart. He used him for his glory. And he described him as a legitimate disciple, a good and righteous man. Remember, those are God's labels, the terms he used to describe Joseph when he was a rich and secret follower, afraid of what he might lose, *before* he stepped forward to claim the body of Jesus.

A HUMBLING THOUGHT

But there's something else that humbles me in this story. It's who's missing.

All of the hard-core Jesus followers who had left everything to follow him are nowhere to be found. These are the guys I used to point to as examples of what it means to radically follow Jesus. But in the darkest moment, when all seemed lost, the courageous lacked courage and the committed showed no commitment. It was only one frightened and secret disciple who stepped up to the plate.

That gives me pause. Serious pause.

First of all, it makes me hesitant to pat myself on the back for any sacrifices I've already made. As they say in investing, "Past performance is no guarantee of future results."

Odds are that I'm not as strong as I think. Jesus' handpicked disciples certainly weren't. It's frightening to realize that the faithful few who had previously stuck with Jesus through thick and thin bailed out as quickly and completely as they did.

It makes me wonder if any of us can lay claim to fully and completely taking up our cross, denying self, and loving him above life itself. I suspect that if truth be told, none of us has a devotion that is as absolute, undivided, or exclusive as we may think it is, even people who trumpet such devotion as the only acceptable mark of genuine discipleship.

Second, it makes me hesitant to call out, write off, or tear apart those who struggle with full devotion and reckless abandonment. Who am I to blast a "secret disciple" as unworthy if Jesus didn't? Who am I to write off the not-yet-fully-committed if Jesus didn't? Who am I to say that God can't use the kind of people he actually used?

Sometimes I wonder if in our quest to purify the church, we've become more like Pharisees than like Jesus. Accidental Pharisees perhaps. But Pharisees nonetheless.

When it comes to bruised reeds, smoldering wicks, and the weary saints, Pharisees have no patience. They pile on heavy burdens and lots of guilt. But they don't lift a finger to make anything easier.[15] They thin the herd at every opportunity.

Not so with Jesus.

The bruised reed he will not break. The smoldering wick he will not snuff out. To the weary and heavily burdened he offers rest, a light load, and an easy yoke.[16]

The beauty of the story of Joseph of Arimathea is that it puts a face on Jesus' compassion, patience, and grace for the struggling saint. Joseph was the ultimate smoldering wick. Many of us would have been tempted to snuff him out. But Jesus fanned his flame. He kept it alive — even if just barely. And eventually the time came when Joseph's little flame burned brighter than all others.

As long as the wick smolders, there is always hope.

We can be like Jesus and fan the flame brighter.

Or we can stomp it out as unworthy, useless, and embarrassing to God.

The choice is ours.

But all I can say is that in the case of Joseph, it's a good thing the flame-stomping crowd didn't get ahold of him first. It would have made a mess out of Easter.

---

15. Matt. 23:4.
16. Matt. 12:20.

Discussion Questions for Part 1

The Dark and Dangerous Side of an Overzealous Faith

1. When it comes to the dark and dangerous side of over-zealous faith, "The problem is not spiritual zeal.... The problem is unaligned spiritual passion, a zeal for the Lord that fails to line up with the totality of Scripture."

   a. Can you think of a time in your life when you were especially zealous for something only to discover later that your zeal didn't line up with the facts?

   b. Can you think of a time in your life when you were especially zealous for something in the spiritual realm only to discover that your zeal didn't line up with Scripture? If so, what happened? What changed your mind? What changes did you make as a result?

2. The Pharisees of Jesus' day were champions of self-discipline, personal sacrifice, and rigid morality. Imagine you were alive back then. How do you think you would have responded to their spiritual passion? Would you

have been inclined to look up to them, be intimidated by them, be repelled by them, or perhaps have some other response? Why or why not?

3. What, if anything, did you find to be most *surprising* in Joseph of Arimathea's story (the "secret disciple" nobody wants to be)?

   a. If you were one of the apostles, how do you think you would have viewed Joseph *before* he boldly stepped forward to claim Jesus' body?

   b. Does his story change anything about the way you look at other Christians? How might it change the way you look at yourself? What does it say to you about the kind of people God uses in his kingdom?

4. If you had to pick just one insight or principle from part 1 to put into practice, what would it be and why?

PART 2

PRIDE

When Comparison
Becomes Arrogance

CHAPTER 4

THE CURSE OF COMPARISON

What T-Ball Taught Me about Pride

I remember when my kids were in T-ball. I tried to coach one of the teams. I'm not sure what was more difficult, teaching the kids to run to first base instead of third or teaching the parents that it didn't matter who won the game.

The kids were mostly five and six years old. Some could barely walk, much less hit or catch. Most had the attention span of a moth. There weren't any scouts with radar guns in the stands. So I'm pretty sure no scholarships were gained or lost. It was supposed to be all about learning the game and having fun. We had a strict rule against keeping score.

But everyone knew the score. Even the kids who could hardly count. If we entered the last inning three runs down and scored four runs, the stands erupted. You would have thought we had won something. But of course no one was keeping score. Well, not officially.

That's when I learned the powerful pull of comparison and the insidious dangers that can come with it. Even when I didn't want to compare and keep score (and really, I didn't want to), I couldn't help it. And neither could anyone else. We all knew.

But the real danger wasn't in our comparisons per se. It was in what we did with the information. We put ourselves and our kids in a pecking order. We felt better or worse about ourselves (and our kids) based on what they did in a game.

If a child hit three home runs, his parents would stand up and shout, "That's my boy!" But if he got hit on the head with a fly ball while chasing a butterfly, they'd hide under the stands.

I know that sounds sick. I mean, it's T-ball. How can we derive even the slightest trace of personal worth or shame from a T-ball game? But we can. And we do. And if you're shaking your head in disgust right now, it's because you've never had your kid hit a grand slam with two outs in the last inning, down by three runs, in a T-ball game.

My kids' T-ball teams taught me how powerful our innate urge to compare is and how quickly we categorize people as winners or losers, based on the flimsiest of reasons. That's bad enough when it comes to T-ball, but it's tragic when it comes to our spiritual life and relationship with the Lord.

THE PROBLEM WITH SPIRITUAL COMPARISONS

Spiritual comparisons are particularly silly. We don't always know the full story. All we see is the outside. There's no way to see the heart. This means that a lot of our conclusions about people are flat-out wrong. As we've already seen, the Pharisees looked impressive on the outside. But they were dead on the inside.

Our spiritual comparisons are also incredibly biased. We have an amazing ability to compare things in a way that causes us to come out on top. And when we come out on top, it's hard not to look down on people who don't measure up.

It's at this point that pride becomes particularly dangerous.

Unfortunately, many of us fail to grasp how dangerous pride is. We know that we shouldn't look down on others, but we tend to see it as a small sin. It's not the kind of thing you go to prison for; it falls somewhere between failing to floss and driving too fast. It's something to work on. But no big deal. Even if we admit to periodic bouts with pride, what most of us mean is, "It's tough staying humble when I'm so much better than everyone else."

I remember once meeting with a group of guys who were passionate about their walk with God. Somehow the conversation turned toward people in the church who were not so passionate. Next thing I knew, they were ripping on the way everyone else raised their kids, spent their money, read their Bible, and set their priorities.

It was one of those "aren't you glad we're not like those guys?" conversations.

Now, these were quality men. They were indeed doing a far better job than most in raising their kids, spending their money, reading their Bible, and setting their priorities. The problem wasn't that they noticed it. The problem was what they did with the information. They used it to justify looking down on everyone else. They became arrogant.

When I called them on it, they were mildly remorseful. Sort of like they'd gotten busted for a speeding ticket. But it was clear that no one felt particularly convicted or was determined not to go there again. So I decided to take them on a little journey through Scripture to see God's perspective on the conversation we'd just had.

We started with Satan's prideful fall and moved on from there. But the shocker for most of them was a list of things God hates. It's found in Proverbs 6:16–19. Right at the top of his "I hate it when you do that" list is "haughty eyes," the disgusted and disdainful look of arrogance that parallels the harsh conversation we'd just had.

There are a lot of things that can anger God. Few people would guess that looking down on others would be at the top of the list. Yet it is. As I told the guys that afternoon, if this passage really means what it says, God would rather have us struggling with porn than with pride.

Now, that got their attention!

But it's true. Their dismissive and judgmental words from earlier in the day weren't minor chitchat. They were major sin. Top-of-the-list sin.

The Unexpected Danger Zone

I've also noticed something strange about this sin that God hates most. It's usually found among people who think they love God most.

Spiritual arrogance is not a back-of-the-line sin; it's a front-of-the-line sin. So much so that sometimes I think of it as an occupational hazard of zealous faith, serious discipleship, and biblical scholarship.

Years ago I was part of an amazing movement of God. I was lucky enough to be at ground zero. I saw everything up close and personal. God's Spirit was at work. Lots of people came to Christ. Lots of lives were radically changed.

But then something happened. We began to compare ourselves with others, and we liked what we saw. We were on fire for God. Most people weren't. So we began to look down on everyone else.

We still loved the lost and the hard-core sinner. But we disdained the less than fully sold-out Christian. We were sure that God was pleased with us and ticked off at them. We assumed that our superior hunger for Scripture and passion for God was the reason why he was pouring out his Spirit so powerfully.

We had no idea that we had arrived at a place of grave spiritual danger. It wasn't long before the movement waned. Too many of us had veered off the path and headed toward a scenic viewpoint called Looking Down on Others.

I have to admit, the view was breathtaking. That's why some of my friends decided to set up camp there. Decades later they still haven't moved. They're living in the past, still certain that God likes them best. They have no idea how much he hates the place where they've chosen to live.

The Ultimate Reward-Killer

Looking down on others is also the ultimate reward-killer. It will nullify a boatload of good deeds and righteous living.[1]

Jesus once told a story about a man with prodigious biblical knowledge, great spiritual discipline, and unquestioned zeal

---

1. Luke 18:9–14.

for God. When he went up to the temple to pray, he was overwhelmed by all that he had accomplished. So he began to thank God that he wasn't like other people. He didn't rob, do evil, or sleep around. He fasted twice a week and tithed off the top.

It was all true. He wasn't blowing smoke. He really was an exceedingly moral man. He had lots to be confident in.

At the same time, another man came into the temple to pray. But he was a loser. He had nothing to offer God. Literally. He was an unscrupulous traitor to his own people. He made his living by collecting exorbitant taxes from his fellow Jews and then passing them on to their Roman oppressors.

As he prayed, he was too ashamed to look up. He stood off in the corner and simply cried out for mercy. And according to Jesus, he got what he asked for.

Now, here is the key to the story you don't want to miss. There is no indication that he cleaned up his act before coming to the temple. Nothing denotes a change in behavior afterward. He apparently came in as a tax collector and went home without a career change. Yet, surprisingly, his prayer was heard. God had mercy on him. In the words of Jesus, he went home "justified."

Imagine that, a traitor and tax collector made right with God.

On the other hand, the Pharisee who had lived such an exemplary life that he'd begun to look down on everyone else had no such luck. His prayers were ignored.

Again, don't miss that.

Star it. Underline it.

According to Jesus, it didn't matter how moral or zealous he was. His arrogant trust in his own righteousness, and his pattern of looking down on everyone else, nullified all the good he had done. It left him worse off than a low-life tax collector.

SO WHO'S ON YOUR LIST?

I've noticed one more thing about arrogance. It's the ultimate blind spot. We never see ourselves as arrogant. We might admit to an occasional struggle with pride, but we never cop to full-blown arrogance. We never think we're inappropriately looking down on others. We think we're seeing things as they really are. We think the people we look down on really are beneath us.

To keep from falling into that trap, I try to regularly ask myself if there is any group of people or Christians for whom I am developing a knee-jerk response of disgust, disdain, or aversion. If the answer is yes, it's an early warning sign that I'm headed down the path of arrogance.

So here's a question you might want to ask yourself: "Do I have my own 'thank God I'm not like them' list? And if so, who's on it?"

If you're passionate about justice, the needs of the poor, and orphans, you probably struggle with people who aren't. Your temptation will be to write them off as uninformed, selfish, or coldhearted. Don't fall for it.

If you live green, care for the planet, recycle, and ride your bike to work, you'll be tempted to look down on those who don't.

If you spend more time than most thinking deeply about theology, read books written by dead guys, and do your Bible study in the original Hebrew and Greek, you'll be sorely tempted to look down on those who think the last book in the Bible is called Revelations, and on those who think the last book in the Old Testament was written by an Italian prophet named Ma-la-chi.[2]

The same goes if you identify yourself as Spirit-led, missional, incarnational, gospel-centered, or some other current Christian buzzword. You'll find it hard not to look down on those who don't even know there's a buzzword to conform to.

I have no idea what tempts you to feel superior. I have no idea what kind of people you're tempted to look down on. But most of us have a list—or at least the beginnings of a list. And most of us have no idea how dangerous that list is. If left in place, it can nullify all the good that we do; it can put us at the top of God's "I hate it when you do that" list.

So if you have one, destroy it. Don't just put it aside in a drawer somewhere. Burn it. Nuke it.

You'll be glad you did. And so will your Lord.

---

2. The last book of the Bible is Revelation—no *s*—and Malachi is usually pronounced "Mal-uh-kye."

CHAPTER 5

PRIDE'S UNHOLY TRINITY

Log-Eye Disease, Self-Deception, and Comparison

To understand how pride sneaks in, we need to recognize its three favorite paths into our lives. Each is toxic enough to kill on its own. Together they make up pride's unholy trinity.

Here's a look at each one, with the goal of recognizing its symptoms and then combating its intrusion into our lives and walk with God.

LOG-EYE DISEASE

Log-eye disease is easy to explain but hard to overcome. It's our natural tendency to see the speck in someone else's eye while being oblivious to the log in our own. It's why we see and remember the worst in others while seeing and remembering only the best in ourselves.

For that, we can thank Adam. Ever since his infamous fall, log-eye disease has been epidemic. So much so that Jesus famously warned us about its dangers when it comes to making judgments about others.[1]

Some time ago I came across a classic example of log-eye disease. It was in an email that was widely circulated on the internet, sent from a woman named Carolyn Bourne to her future daughter-in-law, Heidi Withers.

As you read it, you'll notice the clarity with which Ms. Bourne saw the social failures of her stepson's fiancée. You'll also notice her absolute blindness to her own lack of social graces. I found it rather astounding. See if you don't agree.

Heidi,

It is high time someone explained to you about good manners. Yours are obvious by their absence and I feel sorry for you. Unfortunately for Freddie, he has fallen in love with you and Freddie being Freddie, I gather it is not easy to reason with him or yet encourage him to consider how he might be able to help you. It may just be possible to get through to you though. I do hope so.

If you want to be accepted by the wider Bourne family I suggest you take some guidance from experts with utmost haste. There are plenty of finishing schools around. Please, for your own good, for Freddie's sake and for your future involvement with the Bourne family, do something as soon as possible.

Here are a few examples of your lack of manners:

- When you are a guest in another's house, you do not declare what you will and will not eat—unless you are positively allergic to something. You do not remark that you do not have enough food. You do not start before everyone else. You do not take additional helpings without being invited to by your host.
- When a guest in another's house, you do not lie in bed until late morning in households that rise early—you fall in line with house norms.

---

1. Matt. 7:1–5.

- You should never ever insult the family you are about to join at any time and most definitely not in public. I gather you passed this off as a joke but the reaction in the pub was one of shock, not laughter.
- You should have hand-written a card to me. You have never written to thank me when you have stayed.
- You regularly draw attention to yourself. Perhaps you should ask yourself why.
- No one gets married in a castle unless they own it. It is brash, celebrity style behavior.

I understand your parents are unable to contribute very much towards the cost of your wedding. (There is nothing wrong with that except that convention is such that one might presume they would have saved over the years for their daughters' marriages.) If this is the case, it would be most ladylike and gracious to lower your sights and have a modest wedding as befits both your incomes.[2]

Ouch!

No wonder Ms. Bourne earned the nickname the Future Mother-in-Law from Hell.

There's no question that some of her criticisms were legitimate. In a proper British society, there are things you simply don't do. No doubt Heidi needed to step it up a few notches to obtain the standard of behavior that's acceptable in an upper-crust British family.

I'm also quite sure that Ms. Bourne judiciously followed all the social protocols that she ripped on her future daughter-in-law for breaking. But it did strike me as a bit odd how she failed to take into account some of the other well-known norms of British social life: things like holding your tongue, feigning kindness, and not assuming the role of mom when you're

---

2. As reported in the *Daily Mail* (July 1, 2011) and widely dispersed across the internet, *www.dailymail.co.uk/news/article-2009518/Carolyn-Bourne-Mother-law-hell-sends-email-bride-Heidi-Withers.html*.

the step-mother-in-law to a twenty-nine-year-old—and a fairly recent addition to the family at that.

I would also have thought that her three marriages, a previous live-in stint with a much older gentleman, and an out-of-wedlock child (what she described as a "colorful past") that the tabloids quickly exposed would have given her pause before she hit the send button.[3]

But that's how log-eye disease works. It enables us to keep a detailed list of the sins and shortcomings of others while conveniently ignoring our own.

I don't share this story to rip on an uptight upper-class Brit. Poor Ms. Bourne received more than her share of scorn and grief once her email went viral. I share it simply as a classic example of log-eye disease in action. While her case may be extreme, we all have the same tendency to see and lash out at the failings of others while remaining oblivious to our own long list of sins.

SELF-DECEPTION

When it comes to evaluating our spiritual scorecard, most of us cheat. The kind of cheating I'm talking about is not intentional. It's not like corking my bat or hiding an ace up my sleeve. It's cheating without even knowing I'm cheating. It's the subtle dishonesty of self-deception—the second member of pride's unholy trinity.

Let's admit it. Most of us have a rather inflated view of ourselves. If you doubt me, think of all the tone-deaf auditions for talent shows, and the countless what-were-you-thinking videos that propagate across the internet. They're compelling evidence that the human race has a knack for self-deceptive, wishful (if not delusional) thinking.

Some folks have the opposite form of self-deception. They are too hard on themselves. They have a chronic or pathological

---

3. As reported in the *Daily Mail* (July 9, 2011), *www.dailymail.co.uk/news/ article–2013020/Carolyn-Bourne-mother-law-hell-hits-Politeness-greatest-gift— tramp-hedgerow.html.*

self-hatred. But that's not where most of us live. Most of us, even if we struggle with self-esteem issues, still have an incredibly high view of ourselves.

If you don't believe me, here's a little test to try.

Give the following list to any gathering of people. Ask them to rate themselves in each area, answering the simple question, "Are you above or below average in each of the following areas?"

- My ability to get along with other people
- My honesty
- My work ethic
- My basic intelligence
- My morality

Here's what you'll find. One hundred percent of people will rate themselves as being above average in *every* category.

How do I know?

I've done this many times. It doesn't matter if the group is large or small; I always get the same results. No matter what trait I ask about, everyone puts himself or herself in the top half of the scale (not necessarily at the very top, but always in the top half).

Now, that's rather strange, don't you think?

If I remember my third-grade math correctly, half of us are below average, by definition. I know that's hard to swallow in an age of happy face stickers and trophies for everyone. But it's a fact. It's elementary math.

But here's the real problem. It's not that we won't admit that we're below average in some important areas of life. It's that we flat-out don't believe it. We're like a small-town athlete with no idea of the competition that awaits him in the big city, or modern-day American schoolchildren who think they're international geniuses at math. We really do think we are at or near the top in everything that matters.[4]

It's no wonder that we're prone to look down on others. Our natural tendency toward self-deception causes us to think we're

---

4. *http://abcnews.go.com/Politics/china-debuts-top-international-education-rankings/story?id=12336108* (December 7, 2010).

in the top percentile of everything important. And from that perspective, it's hard not to be a little bit (or a whole lot) arrogant.

COMPARISON

Finally, there's the last member of pride's unholy trinity. It's the urge to compare, which we looked at in the previous chapter.

Again, comparison is not a bad thing per se. It's a rather natural response. We need some level of it to make sense of our world. Without comparison, we couldn't rate or improve anything. We wouldn't know which restaurant is best, which book to buy and which to leave on the shelf. We couldn't know whether a student is progressing on target or starting to fall behind.

But the problem with *spiritual* comparisons is that we can't read hearts. We don't know backgrounds. We don't know whether someone has come a long way or has barely grown. We don't know what God has done behind the scenes or what he has in store for the future.

None of us would have pegged blaspheming Saul as the future apostle Paul.

Or consider Ryan and Connor (two people I know, whose names—and a few key details about them—I've changed to protect their privacy).

Ryan handles conflict amazingly well. He never blows up. He finds common ground. He immediately moves toward a win-win solution.

Connor is a hothead. Conflict brings out the worst in him. He goes for the jugular. He often says things he later regrets.

From the outside looking in, it seems obvious that God is more pleased with Ryan's responses than with Connor's. But there is more to the story. Ryan's calm response is part of his basic makeup. He's been that way from birth. Long before he was a Christian, he was a peacemaker. The fact is, he hasn't changed all that much since coming to Christ. He's pretty much the same guy now as he was then.

Connor, on the other hand, was raised by wolves. He comes from one of the worst family backgrounds I've ever known.

Drunken rage, flashing knives, and occasional gunfire marked the near-daily conflict in his home. He learned to survive by being tougher than the next guy.

His current response to conflict, while far from exemplary, is light-years ahead of where it was when I met him. He's grown a ton—with a few tons still to go.

So with whom is God most pleased? Ryan and his mature, biblical response (even though he hasn't really grown much since coming to Christ) or Connor and his still-hotheaded responses that are a massive improvement over where he was just a few short years ago?

If I'm comparing the two without knowing the whole story, I'll pick Ryan every time. That's why comparison is so silly. It never has all the facts. The truth is, Connor is a poster child for spiritual growth, even though he still has a long way to go.

Ryan and I have no right to look down on Connor the next time he struggles with a volatile situation. We can speak into his life, point out the sin, and hold him accountable. But we'd be fools to look down on him. He's come a lot farther than either of us has.

It doesn't matter what area we're comparing, whether it's our commitment to spiritual disciplines, our financial sacrifices, our theological maturity, our community involvement, our evangelistic zeal, or anything else we choose to use as a spiritual measurement; there is simply too much we don't know to justify looking down on others.

We can't see what God sees, which is why he asks us to leave the judging to him.

CHAPTER 6

OVERCOMING PRIDE

The Proper Use of Scripture and
a Proper Understanding of Obedience

Scripture and obedience are the bread and butter of spiritual maturity. Yet I've found that lots of Christians who revere the Scriptures misuse them in ways that produce more pride than righteousness. The same goes for obedience. Some of the most meticulously obedient folks I've known have also been some of the most prideful.

So how does that happen? How is it possible for the Scriptures and obedience to produce Pharisees instead of disciples?

It all has to do with *how we use* the Bible and *how we interpret* our obedience. Let me explain.

THE PROPER USE OF SCRIPTURE

The Bible is supposed to be used like a mirror. It's meant to show us who God is, what he wants, and how we measure up. When I gaze intently into it and make the changes it calls for, it produces righteousness and blessing.[1]

---

1. James 1:22–25; 2 Tim. 3:16–17.

But some of us use it for other purposes. We use it as a pair of binoculars, treat it as a prop to show off our intellectual prowess, or turn it into a springboard for speculation. None of these uses produces righteousness. All of them foster pride.

The Bible as Binoculars

It's always tempting to use the Bible as binoculars. It's kind of cool to see everyone else's faults in granular detail. It's far less threatening than having to deal with some of the ugly things I might see in the mirror.

I remember once listening to a nationally known leader who was an expert at using the Bible as a pair of field glasses. We were speaking at a conference together. In his talk, he presented an impassioned and harsh critique of the inadequacies of the American church (and most Christians). He pretty much ripped on everyone. Many of his concerns were legitimate, even if his tone was inappropriate.

But a few hours later, in a private conversation, he confided in me that his own marriage was on the rocks. It seems that his wife had shut down, feeling that he was too critical, cold, aloof, and controlling.

So I pointed out some key verses about the priority of our marriages and challenged him to quit worrying about all the problems in the American church, cut down on his travel schedule, and focus on repairing his marriage. He looked at me like I was from Mars. He blew me off as an undiscerning ostrich-head who didn't understand the gravity of the situation in the church today.

I didn't know how to respond. He obviously had no interest in what the mirror of Scripture revealed about his marriage. He found it much more comfortable to focus on the grievous errors of all the churches and pastors he didn't agree with. He had turned his Bible into a powerful pair of binoculars—and his marriage into a mess.

The Bible as a Prop

Another way to avoid looking into the mirror of Scripture is to use it as a prop. Instead of peering into it to see what we need to work on and change, we can use it to show off our intellectual prowess, theological acumen, and superior knowledge.

Biblical knowledge and accurate theology are valuable traits. Right thinking leads to right living, just as stinking thinking leads to stinking living. But as valuable as biblical knowledge is, I think it should come with a warning label. The fact is, the more we know, the more we're tempted to look down on people who don't know what we know.[2]

This is not to say that doctrine is unimportant. There are genuine heresies out there. They need to be exposed. Some teaching can be so off base that it cuts us off from Christ. Just check out Paul's letter to the Galatians for an example. Paul doesn't mince words. He attacks false teaching head-on.[3]

But let's be honest. Most of the biblical and doctrinal points that we love to argue about (and take such pride in knowing) are not matters of salvation. They may be important, but they're not essential. They're not damnable heresies. They're simply wrong-headed interpretations by well-meaning people who've misunderstood a few points in a very big and complex book.

When we use the Bible as a prop, every issue and doctrinal disagreement becomes a flash point, an opportunity to show off our superior knowledge and understanding, a way to set us apart. We forget that the entrance exam to heaven is a blood test, not a Scantron. We forget that pride and a lack of love nullifies our knowledge, even if it's a full and complete understanding of all the mysteries in the Bible.[4]

The Bible as a Springboard

Another way of avoiding the discomfort of looking at ourselves in the mirror of Scripture is to turn the Bible into a springboard for speculation.

---

2. 1 Cor. 8:1: "Knowledge puffs up while love builds up."

3. See particularly Galatians 5:1–12, where Paul points out that those who see circumcision as a requirement for salvation are in danger of cutting themselves off from Christ and falling away from grace.

4. 1 Cor. 13:1–4.

For instance, when I first became a Christian, I was excited to discover all the Bible had to say about God, sin, grace, and how I was supposed to live.

But it wasn't long before my curiosity about how to live was replaced by a less threatening curiosity. I wanted to know who the Antichrist might be, what kind of fish swallowed Jonah, why the disciples on the Emmaus road didn't recognize Jesus, and why God let Satan talk him into messing up Job's life.

The Bible didn't answer any of these questions. But I found lots of teachers, books, and podcasts that claimed to have the answers. I found their theories and speculations to be intellectually stimulating and fun to ponder. For a while I lost myself in them. I became a self-appointed expert on all things unanswerable.

But I was deceived.

The Bible leaves lots of questions unanswered. It wasn't written to answer everything I might want to know about God, the universe, or the unseen realm. Some things are simply beyond my comprehension, unimportant, or none of my business.[5]

The more time and energy I spent trying to answer the unanswerable, seeking to solve every biblical paradox, and digging into complex theological systems that claimed to explain everything that God didn't explicitly spell out in his Word, the more I missed what God was trying to tell me. And the more I became prideful instead of godly.

A PROPER UNDERSTANDING OF OBEDIENCE

Just as the proper use of Scripture is important, so is a proper understanding of obedience.

For years, I misunderstood the role of obedience. I thought I was doing something worthy of praise when I obeyed. I thought that the more carefully I obeyed, the more I was earning God's favor and the rewards that came with it.

The Bible clearly teaches that obedience is rewarded. But it

---

5. Deut. 29:29; Isa. 55:8–9.

also contains a warning about the folly of finding pride in our obedience. It's found in Luke 17:7–10. I remember when I first read it. It rocked my boat.

In this passage, Jesus says that a servant who obeys has done nothing special. Let me say that again. It's too important to miss. *A servant who obeys has done nothing special.* He has simply done his job. When he comes in from the field after completing his chores, his master doesn't jump for joy. He doesn't kill the fatted calf and host a banquet in his honor. He politely thanks him and gives him something else to do.

Here are Jesus' exact words: "So you also, when you have done *everything* you were told to do, should say, 'We are unworthy servants; we have only done our duty'" (v. 10, emphasis added).

My goodness. That sure puts obedience in a different light. It doesn't leave much room for pride and looking down on others as if I've done something special.

Obedience is far better than disobedience. But when I turn my obedience into a source of spiritual pride, it's as ridiculous as one of my sons demanding ice cream and a new bicycle because he didn't cheat on his test, get into a fight at school, or steal any money.

When I obey, God doesn't chest bump with the angels. When my obedience outpaces the obedience of others, I haven't done something worthy of a peacock's strut.

So why is it that so many of us find pride in superior obedience?

I think it's because we misunderstand God's commands. We think of them as difficult and burdensome. We hear sermons and read passages about counting the cost, dying to self, and leaving all behind, and we assume that God's commands are designed to separate those of us who have what it takes to become a true disciple from those who don't.

But God's commands are not burdensome. They're beneficial. With the power of the Holy Spirit, they're not that hard to keep. God gives us both the will and the power to obey. That's why obedience is not above and beyond the call of duty. It is the call of duty. It doesn't turn us into the spiritual equivalent of a Navy

SEAL. It's the natural byproduct of loving Jesus. It's the very definition of being a follower.[6]

When we realize this, it kills the temptation to puff up with pride. It defuses our propensity to look down on people who are still struggling. Once we comprehend that we've done nothing special, there's nothing to boast about.

As we've seen, God hates pride. It's at the top of his "I hate it when you do that" list. But for some reason, lots of us downplay our tendency to pat ourselves on the back and to look down on others, especially if we think of ourselves as being at the front of the following-Jesus line.

But the truth is, pride and looking down on others wrecks everything. It's a cancer that spreads until it kills. If we want to please the Lord and hear, "Well done, good and faithful servant," we need to see it in the mirror and root it out immediately, at all costs.

If not, we'll become a Pharisee—accidentally perhaps, but a Pharisee nonetheless.

---

6. 1 John 5:3; Phil. 2:13.

Discussion Questions for Part 2

PRIDE

1. As we've seen, our spiritual comparisons can be spiritually dangerous. Take a moment to list all of the downsides and dangers you can think of that can come from comparing ourselves with others.

2. It's hard, if not impossible, to avoid making comparisons. They happen naturally and subconsciously.

   a. What are some areas of your life where you are most prone to compare yourself with others?

   b. When you find yourself comparing, are you most likely to focus on areas of your life where you don't match up, or on areas where you tend to come out on top? Why do you think that is?

3. If it's true that we all have a list of people we naturally look down on, what types of people are most likely to end up on your personal, "I'm so glad I'm not like them list"? What do you think Jesus would say to you about your list?

4. How would you advise someone who asked you, "What can I do to avoid 'log-eye disease'?" What specific steps would you suggest they take?

5. Do you think most people are inclined to use the Bible as a mirror, or as a pair of binoculars? Which are you most inclined toward, and why?

6. If you had to pick just one insight from part 2 that has your name on it, what would it be? Why? And how do you plan to respond to it?

PART 3

EXCLUSIVITY

When Thinning the Herd
Becomes More Important
Than Expanding the Kingdom

CHAPTER 7

EXCLUSIVITY

Raising the Bar to
Keep the Riffraff Out

When the church I pastor ran out of seating years ago, we decided to add a Saturday night worship service to the mix. We did it to hold off building more buildings. We also saw it as a great way to reach people who had to work on Sundays.

A couple of days after I announced the new service, I received a note from a member. He was upset that we were making it too easy for people to come to church. He believed that God deserved the bulk of the day. He was already annoyed that we had an early morning service on Sundays, where people could go to church early and then get on with the rest of their day.

In his mind, the best way to guarantee that God got the full day that he deserved was to start worship at the traditional eleven o'clock hour. It grieved this man that we would make attending church more convenient. He thought we were selling out. He believed that stacked parking, uncomfortable chairs, and forcing people to come early to get a good seat were great ways to thin the herd and separate the wheat from the chaff.

His favorite verses were about narrow gates and many being called but few chosen. He also felt that people who weren't willing to make the necessary lifestyle and financial sacrifices to worship on Sunday weren't real Christians. He was convinced that by accommodating their busy schedules, we were giving a false sense of spiritual confidence to people who had no right to be spiritually confident. As far as he was concerned, if they weren't willing to pay the high price of commitment, they didn't deserve to be saved anyway.

When I read his note, I burst out laughing. But another part of me wanted to cry.

I thought his note was funny because he evidently didn't understand the original reasons behind the traditional 11:00 a.m. worship service. It wasn't so that people could give God the bulk of their day. It was a relic of a more rural culture, when people needed to milk the cows before coming to church. Sounds like a rather consumeristic and accommodating way to determine your starting time, don't you think?

But I wanted to cry because this was a man who'd gone to our church for years. He had notebooks full of sermon outlines. Yet he still had no understanding of what biblical grace and mercy were all about. He thought they were earned.

I'd obviously failed as a Bible teacher.

I'm not saying that there's no cost involved in following Jesus. Of course there is. Genuine faith always produces significant changes in our actions, values, and priorities. I would expect anyone who is a mature believer to make corporate worship a top priority no matter how inconvenient it might be.

But that wasn't his point. He wasn't worried about mature Christians. He was concerned that we were making it too easy for the not-yet, new, immature, and struggling Christian. He wanted to keep out the less-than-fully-committed. He thought that would purify the church.

He also thought he was doing the work of Jesus. But he wasn't. He was doing the work of a Pharisee—accidentally, of course.

KEEPING THE RIFFRAFF OUT

I find such thin-the-herd thinking to be widespread today. Everywhere I turn, I find well-meaning speakers, authors, and other highly committed Christians raising the bar (and taking pride in keeping it high) by redefining what it means to be a genuine Christian.

Their teaching seems to suggest that a real Christian is someone who always chooses the harder path and then piles on a bunch of extra burdens for good measure. They call for greater sacrifice, deeper study, more evangelism, tutoring kids, adopting children, digging wells, stopping sex trafficking, living more simply, and a host of other things they see as the proof of genuine discipleship. Their drive-by guiltings can mow down an entire crowd.

You may wonder, "What's wrong with that?" It sounds like a recipe for radically committed Christianity. But it's not. It's a recipe that leaves out lots of important ingredients. It emphasizes a select few favorite verses and teachings from Jesus while pretty much ignoring the rest of the New Testament. It's not a recipe for discipleship. It's a recipe for Phariseeism.

Now, I'm not saying that anyone is *intentionally* trying to produce a brood of Pharisees. In most cases, people who prescribe a more radicalized and activist faith have the best of intentions. They want our churches and people to reach their full spiritual potential. They don't want to settle for mediocrity.

But there is something worse than settling for mediocrity. It's exclusivity. It's the temptation to up the ante and to raise the bar of discipleship so high that it disqualifies all but the most committed, and thus thins the herd that Jesus came to expand.

UNREALISTIC EXPECTATIONS

I know this pattern so well because I've been there. I even have a T-shirt to prove it. I was once a bar-raising pastor. I believed I was helping Jesus out. I assumed he was especially pleased with me. But I was wrong. Terribly wrong.

My expectation that every Christian should become a superstar disciple (radical, passionate, a leader, a Bible scholar, an evangelist, a person who feeds the hungry, practices selfless generosity, and makes a difference overseas) was unrealistic and unbiblical.

I had no room in my theology for Paul's admonition that we

make it our ambition to lead a quiet life, to mind our own business, and to work with our hands.[1] Verses like that made no sense to me. It sounded like a description of a wimpy Christian, the very kind of person I preached against and looked down on. So I put verses like that out of my mind and focused on the ones that fit better with my image of a Christian warrior kicking Satan's butt and advancing the kingdom.

But the result wasn't an advance of the kingdom. It was a heavy load of free-floating guilt. You see, no matter what people did, it was never enough. There was always more to do if we really loved Jesus and wanted to be all he'd called us to be.

MY GOOFY STRATEGY

Like many of my peers, I thought the best way to help people grow spiritually was to stretch them as much as possible. Under the guise of helping them grow, I loaded them down with increasingly heavy burdens. I thought it would make the weak strong.

In my mind, the quest for spiritual maturity was like an onion and a video game.

With regard to sin, it was like an onion. There was always another layer to peel off. If people weren't feeling seriously guilty about something, they obviously weren't listening to the Holy Spirit. I rated Christian books and sermons by how bad they made me feel. The worse I felt, the better the sermon. The more difficult and challenging they were, the more faithful the message.

With regard to growth, it was like a video game. There was always a higher level to attain. No matter how much people grew, no matter what sacrifices they made to get to that point, there was always a next level they needed to reach to fully please the Lord.

Worse, I chided people who grew weary. I pushed them to work harder, pray longer, and study more. Taking a break or temporarily stepping to the sidelines was simply not an option. Satan didn't rest; why should we?

My discipleship motto was simple: no pain, no gain. If you wanted rest, a lighter load, or an easier path, you'd come to the

---

1. 1 Thess. 4:11.

wrong place. I didn't think that's what Jesus offered. He offered a cross to bear, death to self, and eternal rewards to the faithful few who were willing to pay the price and stay the course.

Or so I thought.

In reality, as we saw earlier, if I'd read my Bible a little more carefully, I would have found that Jesus did offer something I had never considered worthy of a Christ follower. He offered rest, a light burden, and an easy yoke to those who were weary and heavily burdened.[2]

Imagine that!

Maybe it's a misprint. Maybe he didn't really mean it.

But then again, maybe that's why he called his message good news. Maybe those of us who constantly demand more are the ones who've missed it.

---

2. Matt. 11:28–30: "Come to me, all you who are weary and burdened, and I will give you rest. Take my yoke upon you and learn from me, for I am gentle and humble in heart, and you will find rest for your souls. For my yoke is easy and my burden is light."

CHAPTER 8

THE REASON JESUS CAME

Why Thinning the Herd Can Be a Bad Idea

For over two thousand years, those who fashion themselves as spiritual leaders haven't been able to leave well enough alone. They keep trying to raise the bar to entry higher than Jesus placed it. They pile on heavier and heavier burdens and call it discipleship. They shut the door to the struggling and weak and call it purifying the church.

Their intentions are noble. But their fruit is rotten. They unwittingly play the same role as the Pharisees of old, trying to keep out the very people Jesus came to reach.

So why do we do that? What tempts someone to want to thin the herd that Jesus came to expand?

THE DESIRE FOR EXCLUSIVITY

The first thing is our fallen human nature. We have a natural bent toward creating and maintaining exclusivity, especially after we've found our own way into the fold. We want to hold on to what we've earned. We want to keep the undeserving out. And sometimes we simply don't want to share what we've gained.

It's a pattern found in virtually every profession. Whether it's hairdressers or accountants, people who are already in the field will sooner or later find a way to raise the standards and entrance requirements to make it harder for others to get in. They will tell you that it's to maintain quality. In reality, it's to cut the competition.

Consider higher education. Most colleges and universities start out with a desire to put education within the reach of the masses. But once they attain a measure of success, they leave the masses behind. They demand higher GPAs and institute tougher entrance requirements in a desire to join the ranks of the elite. The alumni love it. It increases the value of their degree. But ironically, many of them couldn't get in under the new standards.

The same holds true in our neighborhoods. After the pioneers have moved in, they almost always band together to keep the future settlers out. Land developers call it NIMBY (Not In My Back Yard). It shows up as the obligatory lawsuit that's filed anytime someone wants to build on a vacant piece of land. The NIMBY mindset says, "Now that I'm here, we've got just the right amount of people."

Though an outsider can see how self-serving these kinds of behaviors are, people on the inside rarely see it. They really believe that they're maintaining quality, creating a better school, or protecting the neighborhood.

It's no different in the spiritual realm. People who decry low standards of salvation and spiritual maturity tend to forget their own past. And most are unaware that their definition of a genuine and mature Christian bears an uncanny resemblance to their own current walk with God. It's an interesting form of spiritual NIMBY.

But here's the real problem. Such thinking and actions aren't only self-serving; they are also diametrically opposed to the purpose and work of Jesus. They are at odds with the very reason why he came.

WHY JESUS CAME

Jesus didn't come to thin the herd. He didn't come to recruit "special ops" Christians. His goal was to expand the kingdom, to bring salvation to people who previously were excluded. He came to seek and find the lost, including a large group of folks no one else wanted to invite to the party.[1] Everything about Jesus' ministry was designed to make salvation and the knowledge of God *more* accessible.

It started with his incarnation. It included his choice of a backwater place like Galilee to call home, and the motley crew he picked to be his apostles. Nothing about Jesus or his followers was elitist. Everything was common, accessible, and well within the reach of the typical man, woman, or child.

Even at the point of Jesus' death, the heavenly Father sent a message of accessibility. The moment Jesus died, the temple curtain that had isolated the Holy of Holies from everyone but the high priest (and even he could enter only once a year, on the Day of Atonement) was ripped open from the top down. What had once been a symbol of the barrier between God and sinful people suddenly became a symbol of open access for all.

Consider also the language of the New Testament. It was written in *Koine* Greek, which means "common" Greek. It was the language of the marketplace, in much the same way that broken or pidgin English is used around the world today. It was hardly the language of the elite, the educated, or even the primary language of the Jews in Jesus' day. But it was the language everyone understood, Jews and Gentiles alike. So it was the language God chose to use to communicate his message.

Of course, not everyone appreciated Jesus' making things so accessible. The religious elite of his day had spent centuries erecting a complicated spiritual obstacle course. Their extrabiblical rules, traditions, and strict intellectual requirements ensured that only people with the best pedigree, biggest brains, and greatest dedication would make it through. It's no surprise that they didn't take too kindly to Jesus' offering everyone a shortcut.

The religious elite weren't opposed to Jesus being a messiah or a king. They were opposed to the kind of people he included in his kingdom. They fought with him because he kept ignoring *their* definitions of committed spirituality. He refused to let *them*

---

1. Luke 19:10: "The Son of Man came to seek and to save the lost."

pick and choose who was going to be invited into the kingdom—and on what basis they would be allowed to come in. So they wrote him off and tried to kill him.

The same thing still happens today. People who plead for stricter and stricter standards of discipleship in the name of a purer church are happy to have a Savior—as long as they can decide whom he saves.

The Crowds That Followed Jesus

Listening to some folks, you'd get the idea that Jesus was always thinning the herd. They take a few isolated statements and incidents from his life and turn them into his standard stump speech.

But the truth is that Jesus did far more to attract huge crowds than he did to shoo them away. And let's be honest. The crowds didn't come because they were hungering and thirsting for God. They came for the same reason most of us would have come: because they'd heard rumors of a holy man who healed the sick, gave sight to the blind, cast out demons, cured lepers, and even raised the dead.[2]

That will draw a crowd.

When those crowds came to see him, Jesus didn't chew them out for their mixed motives. He didn't chide them for selfishly seeking miracles. He didn't sneak off to the desert to see if they were still committed enough to come out and find him.

It was just the opposite. He had compassion on them. He healed their sick. He told them about the kingdom. He called them to righteousness. Then he moved on to the next town to do it all over again.

And the crowds were fickle. Incredibly fickle. Most returned home right after the show was over. There is little evidence that many were profoundly changed or converted. When they thought he might deliver them from the Romans, they cried out, "Hosanna!" But when it became obvious that he wasn't interested in overthrowing the Romans, they cried out, "Give us Barabbas!"

Yet Jesus continued to pursue the masses. He didn't write

---

2. Matt. 4:23–25.

them off, even though he knew their hearts and the inevitable endgame. He continued to give them undeserved chance after undeserved chance. Certainly, he thinned the herd a time or two, once to the point that so few were left that he asked the twelve disciples if they were going to leave too.[3] But that was *not* his normal pattern. It was a onetime sermon.

Many people who long for a more radicalized church miss this. They place their emphasis on the difficulty and challenge of following Christ rather than on the good news of his burden-bearing grace. And when they do speak of his great love, it's primarily as a motivation for us to do more—and a reason why those who do less aren't worthy to be included. People who feel this way don't realize it, but they want a church that looks a lot more like the ministry of John the Baptist than the ministry of Jesus Christ.

JESUS OR JOHN THE BAPTIST?

John the Baptist played hard to get. He hung out in the desert, wearing funky clothes and eating strange food. Under a Nazirite vow from birth, he was what we would today call an ascetic—someone characterized by self-discipline and the commitment to abstain from all forms of self-indulgence.

Large crowds came to hear him. But to do so, they had to make a difficult trek into the wilderness. That alone separated the window-shoppers from the serious seekers.

He also had a major thin-the-herd message. In essence, John told the people who showed up that they were going to hell. He told them that if they didn't repent and get baptized for their sins (something Jews thought only Gentiles had to do to get right with the God of Abraham, Isaac, and Jacob), they were doomed and would suffer the judgment of God. Even more astounding, John told the religious leaders the very same thing. Maybe that's why they weren't too fond of him.

But Jesus' ministry was radically different.

---

3. John 6:60–67. This occurred at the conclusion of Jesus' famous Bread of Life message (John 6:25–59).

While Jesus wasn't afraid to say hard things and draw lines in the sand, he didn't hide out in the wilderness. He went toward the people. He made it easy for them to hear him. He did things designed to draw huge crowds. He even healed people *before* they made a commitment to follow him. His entire life and ministry had such a populist tone that the religious elite wrote him off as profane. They falsely accused him of being a glutton and a drunkard. Even John the Baptist was confused by Jesus. John eventually sent some of his own disciples to double-check: was Jesus really the promised Messiah?[4]

I find that amazing, because if anyone should have been certain that Jesus was the Son of God, it was John. After all, when he baptized Jesus, he saw the Holy Spirit alight on him like a dove and then heard the Father say, "This is my Son, whom I love; with him I am well pleased."[5]

That's pretty straightforward. There's not much ambiguity there. I think that would be hard to forget. Yet apparently Jesus' ministry with the crowds was so different from what a radical ascetic like John expected that it caused him to wonder if perhaps he'd gotten it all wrong.

Many of today's spiritual elite seem to wonder the same thing. Presented with a Jesus-style ministry that attracts large crowds of spiritually uncommitted what's-in-it-for-me window-shoppers (and then meets their needs and teaches them the counsel of God in a palatable way that leaves them longing for more), the spiritual elite write it off as a compromised ministry with a watered-down gospel.

The thin-the-herd crowd even has a derisive name for the people who attend these churches. They call them consumer Christians. And woe to the ministry or church that does anything designed to reach out to them or keep them around for a while. So we'll need to look at them next.

---

4. Luke 7:18–35. John and his disciples were clearly confused by the way Jesus went about his public ministry.

5. Matt. 3:16–17.

CHAPTER 9

THE SINNERS JESUS LIKED TO HANG AROUND

Why "Consumer Christians" Deserve a Little Love

The word on the street is that some believers actually select a church based on what it does for them. Imagine that!

To the religious elite, this is horrifying. They can't fathom Jesus being pleased with a churchful of people who decided where to worship based on a preferred worship style or a preacher they can connect with. They think it's awful that so many Christians decide where to go to church based on the quality of the children's and youth programs rather than the opportunities for missional and community ministry.

You'll find these so-called consumer Christians clustered in two kinds of churches. They attend traditional churches that do church in a comfortable and nostalgic "this is how it's always been done" way. And they attend supersized megachurches that cater to their desires with top-notch bands, interesting speakers, air-conditioning that actually works, and parking attendants who make sure no one has to wait too long to get in or get out.

To my thinking, these consumer Christians are the modern-day equivalent of the crowds that followed Jesus. They're fickle. They flock to the latest and greatest. Many of them don't get it. Many will abandon ship at the first sign of hardship. While these are hardly admirable traits, they are remarkably similar to the traits found in the people Jesus had compassion for and doggedly pursued for the full three years of his public ministry.

Yet today's religious elite view them with derision and scorn. They chalk them up as selfish pigs. They note their carnal pursuit of a what's-in-it-for-me Savior and write them off as unworthy, shooing them away or, better yet, doing their best to keep them from ever showing up in the first place.

THE ULTIMATE "UNCOMFORTABLE" CHURCH

I remember talking to a young pastor who was convinced that Jesus would be most pleased if he could get his church to the point that it was made up exclusively of fully committed Christians. He didn't mind some hard-core sinners showing up. They deserved to hear the gospel a first time. But he didn't want any consumer Christians. They'd already had too many chances.

A big part of his plan was to build the ultimate *uncomfortable* church.

Really.

After reading a number of books and hearing some stirring talks at conferences, he had come to the conclusion that it was ridiculous to spend money on snazzy church buildings that lured the uncommitted masses, when Christians in other parts of the world were willing to meet for hours under the shade of a tree.

He told me, "If persecuted Christians walk for miles and meet at great personal peril in harsh and cramped secret settings, why can't we show the same kind of commitment? Why do we need fancy buildings, when we could use the money to help those in need? Why can't we meet in a tent or a tilt-up? Why can't we sit on folding chairs or on the floor?"

Then he hit me with what he thought was the coup de grâce.

"If Green Bay Packer fans can sit for hours in the freezing cold cheering on their favorite team, why can't we do the same for Jesus?"

Unfortunately, he overlooked something rather important.

He forgot who shows up at Lambeau Field in the middle of winter.

It's filled with people who are *already* rabid Packer fans.

I'm from San Diego. If I moved to Green Bay and you wanted to convert me into a Packer fan, you'd better get me a flat-screen. There's no way I'm going to the game if it's less than fifty degrees outside.

Should you trick me into going (by emphasizing the excitement and lying about the ten-degree windchill factor), I guarantee you I'd be in a taxi by halftime. The result would not be a new Packer fan.

If our goal is to fill our churches with *only* people who are already deeply committed to Jesus, then it might be a good idea to build a Lambeau Field – type worship facility. But if our goal is to persuade the unconvinced, reach out to the uninitiated, and invite the not-yet-interested to come and see what Jesus and Scripture is all about, it might be a good idea to make our buildings (whether they be house churches or megachurches) as inviting and comfortable as possible.

THE SINNERS JESUS LIKED TO HANG AROUND

The notion that consumer, casual, and cultural Christians need to be smoked out and driven away at the first opportunity ignores something significant about the ministry of Jesus. The sinners that Jesus so famously liked to hang around were not hard-core pagans who had never been exposed to God's Word. The prostitutes, tax collectors, and others who so irritated the Pharisees were almost exclusively Jews who knew the ways of God but, for whatever reason, chose not to follow them.

Perhaps they presumed upon their religious heritage or their Abrahamic covenant. Perhaps they felt that even though their sins were great, at least they weren't as bad as the heretical Samaritans and the idol-worshiping Gentiles.

Who knows?

But one thing is certain: in an environment where cultural, religious, and ethnic identities were so intertwined, there is no way these "sinners" were ignorant of God's law. Their sins weren't sins of ignorance. They knew what they were doing. That's why Jesus could tell them to stop sinning without having to explain further. They knew exactly what he meant.

That sounds an awful lot like the situation we face in many of our churches today. They're filled with people who are presuming upon their religious heritage, a casual belief in Jesus and the resurrection, or a prayer they prayed at seventh-grade summer camp.

The thin-the-herd crowd wants us to write these people off as unworthy of our time, energy, or compassion. They want us to focus instead on the hard-core pagans rejected by the church and society. But we can't redefine the ministry of Jesus so that it fits our paradigm. If we want to reach out to sinners like Jesus did, then our list of approved sinners will also have to include the carnal, cultural, and consumer Christians who populate our pews.

Now, don't get me wrong. I am not saying that we should be satisfied with a church full of casual, carnal, or consumer Christians. I'm not saying that we should settle for a definition of spiritual maturity that's nothing more than a nod to God. I'm not saying we should ignore church discipline in the face of continuing sin.[1]

Our ultimate goal can be nothing less than full obedience to *everything* Jesus taught. It's the only way we can fulfill the second half of the Great Commission.[2] But our attitude toward people

---

1. 1 Corinthians 5:11–13 gives a specific list of sins that are grounds for spiritual separation when practiced by self-proclaimed Christians. If such people fail to repent, the passage says, we are not to associate with them unless or until they do so.

2. Matt. 28:18–20. The Great Commission ends with a command to teach disciples to obey everything Jesus commanded. Colossians 1:28–29 describes the goal of the apostle Paul's ministry: to present everyone perfect in Christ.

who struggle and even ignore what they already know needs to be aligned with the compassion and ministry of Jesus rather than the disdain, disgust, and exclusivity of the Pharisees.

But that raises one more question.

Aren't these people really just lukewarm Christians? Didn't Jesus say somewhere that he hates lukewarm Christians?

THE LUKEWARM CHURCH IN LAODICEA

Like many, I once justified my disgust with struggling and half-hearted Christians by referring to Jesus' words to a lukewarm church in Laodicea. In the third chapter of Revelation, Jesus tells the Laodiceans that he'd rather have them hot or cold — anything but lukewarm. He goes on to say that he will spew them out of his mouth if they don't get their act together.[3]

To me, this passage was crystal clear. God hates it when we're lukewarm in our faith. People who claim to know him but fail to follow him with full passion belong in a spittoon. But I had missed something important.

Jesus wasn't suddenly switching gears in this passage. After an earthly ministry of reaching out and pursuing the less-than-fully-committed, he wasn't abruptly writing them off now that he was back in heaven. He was still pursuing.

Despite their tepid faith, Jesus wasn't slamming the door in their face. He was doing the opposite. He was pleading with them one more time, counseling them to buy from him what they didn't even realize they needed. He stands at the door knocking, in the hope that someone will open it and let him back into his own church.

This is a rebuke motivated by love, not by loathing. The Laodiceans were incredibly messed up. They were not only luke-warm; they were arrogant about it. They thought they were rich. They thought they needed nothing. In reality, as Jesus said, they were "wretched, pitiful, poor, blind and naked" (v. 17).

---

3. Rev. 3:14–22.

But Jesus didn't give up on them. He warned them one more time in the hope that they would come to their senses. They'd apparently been lukewarm for a long time. Yet he still pursued. The time would come when he would spit them out. But the time had not yet arrived.

Whenever our passionate pursuit of radically committed Christianity results in writing off or shooing away or otherwise taking it upon ourselves to spit out people who lag behind (even way behind), something has gone terribly wrong. We can no longer claim to be aligned with the heart of Jesus. At that point, we've crossed the line. We've become part of the spiritual elite—an accidental Pharisee.

The truth is that Jesus didn't come to raise the bar. He didn't come to weed out the losers. He came to turn losers, laggards, and enemies into full-on sons and daughters of God.

He will judge, and it won't be pretty when he does. But he prefers to pursue and to forgive. That's why he cried out on the cross, "Father, forgive them, they do not know what they do." That's why he warned the Laodiceans one last time. That's why he still hasn't come back in fiery judgment.

Jesus is not slow in keeping his promise to return and judge. He's patient. He doesn't want any to perish, but *everyone* to come to repentance.[4] And that includes the hard-core sinner, the lukewarm, and even so-called consumer Christians. That's why I find our current disdain for the less-than-fully-committed so perplexing.

I think Jesus does too.

---

4. 2 Peter 3:7–9.

Discussion Questions for Part 3

Exclusivity

1. As you look at the churches and Christians you personally know, are there any areas where you believe the bar needs to be raised in terms of what it means to follow Jesus? If so, list them. What makes these things particularly important?

2. Have you ever found yourself drawn toward an expression of Christianity that emphasized "thinning the herd" more than "expanding the kingdom"? If so, what are some of the areas and issues you focused on? How would you respond differently today?

   a. As we saw, a bias toward (or a delight in) thinning the herd is spiritually dangerous and out of line with Jesus. If you had to confront someone who preferred thinning the herd to expanding the kingdom, what would you say to them?

   b. Obviously, there is a time and a place to thin the herd. Jesus did so. Can you think of some areas today where we need to thin the herd?

3. Have you ever experienced or observed the NIMBY effect (Not In My Back Yard) in your own church, small group, or circle of Christian friends? What happened? What can you learn from that experience?

4. Would you agree that, at some level, we are all "consumer" Christians? Why or why not? And is that a good thing, a bad thing, or no big deal?

5. Looking back over the chapters in part 3, what one thing most jumps out at you as something you had never seen before or you need to work on most? What makes that particular principle or insight important? How do you plan to respond to it?

PART 4

LEGALISM

When Sacrifice Crowds Out Mercy

CHAPTER 10

THE NEW LEGALISM

The Danger of Litmus Test Christianity

Pharisees love a litmus test. Always have. Always will.

In the days of Jesus, their rigid rules and extrabiblical standards gave them a quick and easy way to distinguish between the godly and the ungodly, the committed and the uncommitted. It allowed them to know who was in and who was out.

For a Pharisee, the most important thing was to be numbered among the spiritually elite. Their worst nightmare was to be stuck in the middle of the pack, numbered among the commoners. Their self-worth was inextricably tied to their ability to differentiate themselves from others. They assumed that only the elite could earn God's favor. So they came up with lots of boundary markers and litmus tests to prove to themselves and to others that they were indeed more committed than most.

A NAME TO BE PROUD OF

Even the name *Pharisee* pointed to their desire to be seen as different. It literally means "separated one." It was a label they wore with honor. It reminded everyone that they were no ordinary Israelites.

Two thousand years later, not much has changed. Those of us who want to be numbered among the highly committed still hate the idea of being average and ordinary. It scares us to death. We assume that God's favor is reserved for the most dedicated. We can't imagine a kingdom of God with room for stragglers, strugglers, doubters, or the weak. So we've created a new set of litmus tests and boundary markers to show that we're still at the front of the line.

But one thing has changed big-time. No one wants to be called a Pharisee anymore. The word no longer connotes the idea of being different and separate. It now signifies someone who is self-righteous and hypocritical. So we've come up with new phrases to describe ourselves as more committed than most. We've coined words like *radical, crazy, missional, gospel-centered, revolutionary, organic*, and a host of other buzzwords to let everyone know that our tribe is far more biblical, committed, and pleasing to the Lord than the deluded masses who fail to match up.

ASKING THE WRONG QUESTION

I understand the desire to be at the front of the pack. High-commitment Christianity is where I want to live. It's where my roots are. It's what I want to see when I look in the mirror. I share the core theology and passion of most of the groups listed above.

But I've also grown increasingly concerned by the proliferation of new boundary markers and litmus tests. I regularly have people ask me if our church is missional, gospel-centered, Spirit-led, expositional, externally focused, and a variety of other terms. No one asks me if we love Jesus. That's too generic. They want to know if I pass their particular litmus test. They want to know if I share their vision, agenda, and code words. If I do, I get the secret handshake. If not, they pray for me.

Litmus test Christianity is never a good thing. It causes us to ask the wrong questions. It pits one part of the body of Christ against another. It plays to pride, fosters exclusivity, and flows out of a heart of legalism. I'm concerned that the new boundary markers and litmus tests of today are not leading us back to New

Testament Christianity; they're leading us back to New Testament Phariseeism. They're simply the newest iteration of old-school legalism.

OLD-SCHOOL LEGALISM

I grew up under old-school legalism and know it well. Our leaders were more concerned with what was in our refrigerator than what was in our heart. Beer or wine would send us to hell, but a critical and slanderous spirit was merely a character flaw to work on.

There were other rules as well. We called them the "dirty dozen." At the top of the list were prohibitions against movie theaters, dancing, and playing cards (at least the kind you could play poker with). We also had a stringent dress code. Short dresses, long hair, and beards were of the Devil, though Jesus seemed to get a special exemption on the long hair and beard rule.

It's a list that most Christians scoff at today. We shake our heads with a tsk-tsk. We wonder why anyone would ever think that an outdated dress code, a boring diet, and short hair could make us better Christians or give us a stronger testimony. Most of us long ago realized that these kinds of rules and regulations have no power in restraining fleshly indulgences, and they certainly can't tell us who's right with God and who isn't.[1]

But the demise of old-school legalism hasn't meant the end of legalism. It's still alive and well. It has deftly morphed into new strains, each with its own set of rules and standards.

THE NEW LEGALISM

The new legalism no longer cares what's in your fridge. It cares what's in your driveway.

Nowadays you can gain some serious street cred if you have the right microbrew in your refrigerator. You'll be written up in Christian magazines as culturally hip if you do your evangelizing in a pub. Movies are no longer evil; they're a source of culturally relevant sermon illustrations. As for dancing, a good DJ has

---

1. Col. 2:20–23.

become as important as a good photographer at many Christian weddings.

Instead the new legalism has a completely different set of standards. Each brand of high-commitment Christianity has its own take on which of these standards are most important and which are nonnegotiable. Each has its own litmus tests.

Here are some examples. You might recognize yourself, your tribe, or some of your best friends. I know I do.

Radical Christians

Radical Christians tend to see generosity as the leading indicator of what it means to follow Jesus. The required metric is a generous and simple lifestyle—with the caveat that if you don't live simply enough, you aren't generous enough.

Unfortunately, the Bible doesn't define what simple living looks like. It doesn't even command it. So self-appointed "radicals" have had to define what is appropriately simple and what is suitably generous. While no one wants to be too detailed or specific (because that might come off as legalistic), I can tell you this: if you have a big house or drive a fancy car, you won't qualify.

A luxury car in the driveway or an expensive house is to a radical what cold beer in the refrigerator is to an old-school legalist. It's proof positive that your priorities are messed up. There's no need to ask more questions. Your possessions make it obvious. You need to get right with God.

Crazy Christians

A second group of highly committed Christians includes people who see themselves as crazy in love with Jesus. Their litmus test of a true disciple is costly personal sacrifices, financial or otherwise. Evidence that you've been persecuted for your faith is highly valued; so are a few wild leaps of faith that all of your friends thought were nutso.

Be aware that if you haven't intentionally chosen some paths of suffering, your commitment to Jesus will be seriously questioned. If your ultimate goal is to live a quiet and peaceful life, minding your own business, don't even bother to apply. You'll be pegged as something less than a true believer (though the apostle Paul might not agree with that assessment).[2]

Missional Christians

A third group of highly committed Christians have adopted the label *missional*. They want to know what you're doing to help fulfill the mission of God. If you start up a soup kitchen, volunteer to tutor at-risk kids, or move your family from the suburbs to the inner city, you'll have no problem earning the badge.

But be forewarned. If you attend a so-called seeker church, you'll have a hard time being accepted into the club. Missional Christians tend to assume that churches with big buildings, large budgets, or extravagant outreach events have compromised with the culture. The same goes for the people who attend them. It's guilt by association.

Gospel-Centered Christians

A fourth group of highly committed Christians are people who choose the moniker *gospel-centered*. They like to determine spiritual maturity by means of their theological grid. If you like big words, careful distinctions, and nuanced debates, you'll fit right in. It also helps if you've read something by Jonathan Edwards recently.

To pass their litmus test, you'll want to use lots of Bible verses, avoid the word *pragmatic*, and tie everything to the gospel. To be certified as spiritually mature, you'll need a robust theology. Of course, that usually demands a robust intellect and a decent education, so if you're slow on the uptake, dyslexic, action oriented, better with your hands than with your mind, or have a hard time with big words and long paragraphs, you'll be allowed to attend,

---

2. 1 Thess. 4:11. The apostle Paul advocated that the Thessalonians make it their ambition to lead a quiet life, minding their own business. However, it appears that most modern-day high-commitment Christian leaders don't think he really meant it.

but don't expect to lead anything. You'll never pass muster as a mature and dedicated disciple.

Revolutionary and Organic Christians

Finally, there are people who like to think of themselves as revolutionary or organic Christians. If you've been deeply hurt or disillusioned by the failings of a large church (or any institutional expression of the church), you are a likely candidate. It's a prerequisite to be keenly aware of the flaws of the established church.

That said, to be fully accepted, you'll have to start attending a house church. If you currently attend a church with a building, mortgage, and paid staff (perhaps because your kids love the youth programs or all of your friends are there), don't worry; you won't have to ditch it immediately. You can begin earning your revolutionary and organic stripes by publically criticizing the church's budget or leadership or by sending some or most of your tithes and offerings elsewhere, so as not to feed the beast.

All of these expressions of the Christian faith are trying to emphasize something good. They all have an important place in the kingdom. But they're all teetering on the edge of a dangerous cliff.

That's because the moment we allow our personal passion and calling to become the litmus test and shibboleth by which we decide who is and who isn't a genuine disciple, we've taken a step too far.[3] At that point, we're no longer building the kingdom; we've started to tear it down. We've become new-school legalists.

---

3. Judg. 12:5–6. When the Gileadites, who were at war with the Ephraimites, captured the fords of the Jordan leading to Ephraim, they asked everyone who wanted to cross over to say, "Shibboleth." If a man said, "Sibboleth" (without the *sh* sound), they knew he was an Ephraimite, because they could not pronounce the word correctly. So they seized him and killed him.

CHAPTER 11

Extra Rules
and Extra
Fences

The Danger of Adding to God's Word

Not long after I became a Christian, I became aware that there were two types of Christians, the basic stripped-down model and the gold package with lots of extra bling.

The stripped-down model went to church, tried to avoid the big sins, and occasionally served as a volunteer somewhere.

Gold-package Christians also went to church and tried to avoid the big sins, but they didn't just volunteer; they served in a leadership capacity. They also had an extensive set of extra-credit rules and tall fences.

Gold-Package Rules

The gold-package rules were designed to foster spiritual maturity. They were mostly centered on spiritual disciplines. Gold-package Christians didn't just pray; they prayed at the right time in the right way. I quickly learned that getting up early in the morning to read my Bible and pray was far more praiseworthy than sleeping in and reading it on the fly. It was also important to write down my observations in a journal, preferably one with a cool leather cover.

They also had lots of other rules. While none were spelled out in the Bible, they were mandatory if I wanted to be counted among the highly committed. They had to do with things like how much television I watched, the importance of family devotions, giving enough money to the right kinds of charities, sharing my faith with strangers, and being conversant with all the hot-button Christian topics of the day. Of course, that's just a partial list. The full list was long and constantly updated.

GOLD-PACKAGE FENCES

The gold-package fences were designed to keep sin out. None of them were found in the Bible, but they were all based on the Bible. In essence, they were extra fences put around God's fences so that nobody would get close enough to the cliff to fall over.

I remember once asking my pastor why we had so many extra fences that weren't in the Bible. He told me they were for our safety. Apparently, God's fences weren't good enough. So we added some extra ones to help him out.

For instance, God had a fence that said, "Don't get drunk," so we added one that said don't drink. He had another fence that said, "Don't fornicate," so we added one that said don't dance. He also had one that said, "Don't love money," so we added one that limited the size of the house you could live in and the price of the car you could drive. We had lots of other fences as well.

It didn't take me long to sign up for the gold package. I wanted to be the best Christian possible. The extra rules and fences provided a track to run on and a great way to show God and everyone else that I was serious about following Jesus.

I gave it my best shot. But I noticed that all the rules and fences didn't do much to make me more like Jesus. I still struggled with all the same sins as did the stripped-down model. Well, actually, I had one more to deal with: pride. It's hard to be humble when you're a gold package surrounded by a lot of stripped-down models.

ADDING TO GOD'S WORD

One thing that makes legalism so dangerous is that it always flows out of the best of intentions. Legalists never see themselves as legalists. They see themselves as obedient. They never think of their extrabiblical rules as extrabiblical. They consider them to be profoundly biblical, the careful application of all that the Bible implies.

When Implications Become Commands

One of the first signs of legalism is a heightened emphasis on the *implications* of Scripture rather than the explicit *commands* of Scripture.

Let's take a command from one of Paul's letters to the Corinthians as an example. In his first letter, he told them to stay morally pure because their bodies were temples of the Holy Spirit.[1]

That's pretty straightforward. But when a budding legalist gets ahold of a passage like this, he'll see far more than just a command to keep our pants on. That's too simplistic. It's not that he'll disagree with the need for moral purity. That's a given. But it's not enough. He'll also want to know what else this passage might imply, how to make sure that he's not missing anything, and how to take his obedience to the next level.

So he's likely to read into it a biblical mandate for physical fitness, a prohibition against body art, piercings, and plastic surgery, or a directive to always look our best, dressed for success, color coordinated, with our teeth flossed.

The Logic of Legalism

On one level, these kinds of extra applications make sense. That's why it's always hard to argue with a legalist. Their rules and fences are always based on the logical extension of a biblical command or principle.

---

1. 1 Cor. 6:15–20. In this passage, Paul is exhorting the Corinthians to cease their immorality, in particular, ritualistic visits to pagan temple prostitutes as a part of fertility rites.

For instance, from a legalist's perspective, if our body is the temple of the Holy Spirit, it's not too much of a stretch to assume that God wants us to treat it with the utmost care. So a passage like this becomes a biblical admonition to exercise regularly, eat right, and get plenty of sleep. It also becomes an indictment of fat people, who are obviously spiritually undisciplined and outside of God's will (unless their name happens to be Spurgeon or D. L. Moody).

The same rationale results in a prohibition against body art, piercings, and plastic surgery. If you wouldn't deface the temple in Jerusalem with graffiti or rearrange the tabernacle, why would you deface or remodel the temple of the Holy Spirit? So this passage becomes a command to leave your body alone.

As for always looking our best, dressed for success? If we're carrying around the Holy Spirit, doesn't it make sense that we'd want to always look our best? It's hard to imagine the Lord being happy with a shoddy temple. In fact, in the book of Haggai, that's exactly what he complained about. The people were fixing up their houses but letting the temple fall into disrepair. He told them to fix it up. Can we do any less with the temple of the Holy Spirit?[2]

Frankly, I'm not sure what the apostle Paul would think of all this. I'm certain he would be surprised to learn that his appeal to the Corinthians to quit visiting temple prostitutes and to stay morally pure also included a directive to get in a good cardio workout, eat organic foods, visit the dentist, and line up a top-notch haberdasher. But that's how legalism works. It takes our desire to be scrupulously faithful to Scripture and turns it into subtle additions to Scripture. It focuses our attention on what we think Scripture means rather than what it actually says.

THE LOSS OF FREEDOM

One of the worst things about this kind of implication-based approach to Scripture is what it does to our freedom in Christ. It destroys it. Let's see how.

---

2. Hag. 1:1–5.

There are lots of legitimate implications that can be drawn from Scripture. The Holy Spirit has probably prompted you to apply some of them to your life. That's one way God takes us to a deeper level in our walk with him. But the moment my personal application of the implications of Scripture becomes the lens through which I judge others, something has gone terribly wrong.

The black-and-white commands of Scripture aren't open to differing interpretations. We don't have the freedom to pick and choose which of the Bible's commands we like and which ones we don't, which ones we agree with, and which ones we find outdated. We don't have freedom to lie, steal, slander, turn a deaf ear to the poor, hoard the gospel, worship idols, or fornicate.

But we do have freedom in many other areas. And it's this freedom that can drive the fledgling legalist within all of us crazy. Once the Holy Spirit places a clear call on our life to do something (or not do it), it's hard for most of us to fathom why everyone else didn't get the same memo.

The same thing happens with Scriptures and issues we've studied carefully. If we've meticulously researched an issue, thought deeply about it, prayed about it, and believe God has revealed something to us, most of us assume that everyone else who is led of the Spirit and intellectually honest with the text will come to the same conclusion. We can't imagine God being pleased with two opposing applications of one Scripture.

Yet as shocking as it may be to some of us, one Scripture can have two opposing applications. Far more often than most of us realize. And coming to grips with this fact can be incredibly difficult. Which explains why we so easily vilify, denigrate, and separate from brothers and sisters with whom God is well pleased, over issues that he doesn't consider all that important.

It's nothing new. The early church fell into the same trap. Their hot-button issues were different. Their battles were over diet and worship. But their goofy thinking and inappropriate responses were remarkably similar to our own. Each side had its favorite texts and arguments to prove its point. Each side wanted to know the *right* answer.

Diet Wars

Some believed that it was deplorable to eat meat that had been offered to an idol. They pointed to Old Testament verses forbidding the worship of idols. They reasoned that eating anything offered to a demon god was an indirect participation in a pagan sacrifice. Since much of the meat sold in the marketplace passed through the pagan temples, they were convinced that the only prudent thing to do was to avoid eating meat rather than to chance it.

Others thought such rules were silly. They pointed to passages declaring idols to be nothing but powerless man-made images. They argued that the command to avoid idol worship had nothing to do with eating a piece of meat that may or may not have been offered to a pagan idol by someone else.

Sabbath Wars

The other battle was over the proper response to the Sabbath. The two sides vehemently disagreed over whether Gentile Christians were required to keep the Jewish Sabbaths.

Many Jewish Christians believed that observing the holy days was a nonnegotiable. They could point to many passages in the Old Testament that commanded God's people to keep the Sabbath holy, as well as to others that detailed the calamities that befell the nation of Israel when they failed to do so.

Lots of Gentile Christians disagreed. They argued that Jesus had fulfilled the Old Testament laws (including the Sabbath laws). They saw no reason why they had an obligation to obey Jewish laws, especially laws that were powerless to save.

A Surprising Answer

When the apostle Paul wrote to settle the dispute, he gave the one answer no one expected. He told them that God was good with all of their answers. He was fine with people who ate meat offered to idols. He was pleased with those who stuck to vegetables. He was good with those who scrupulously kept all the Jewish Sabbaths, and he was pleased with those who treated every day alike.

For Paul, it was a matter of freedom in Christ. The Bible

didn't spell out any instructions about eating meat offered to idols and didn't address Gentile adherence to the Jewish Sabbaths, so they were free to figure it out on their own, as led by the Holy Spirit and guided by their conscience.

But there was one thing God wasn't pleased with. It was the disrespect each side showed the other. Apparently, the more rigid believers were *judging* people who ate meat and treated every day alike, while those who were more laid back *looked with contempt* upon those whom they considered to be uptight and unnecessarily strict.

Paul told both sides to back off.[3]

Don't miss the distinction between judging people and showing contempt. It is important. It still happens today. Those of us who have a bent toward a rigid and rule-based expression of our faith tend to judge and condemn those who don't follow our rules or match up to our standards. At times, we can even wonder if they are genuinely saved. Meanwhile those of us who consider these rules and standards unnecessary tend to look with disgust and contempt upon those who insist on keeping them. We chalk them up as uptight and narrow-minded.

According to Paul's exhortation, both responses are dead wrong.

We have no right to judge people whom God accepts.

We have no right to look with contempt upon people whom God loves.

Learning to Figure It Out

Even the explicit commands of Scripture can leave room for a nuanced application that we'll have to figure out on our own.

For instance, the story of the good Samaritan commands us to love our neighbor as ourselves and makes it clear that the definition of *neighbor* includes even our perceived enemies. I can't limit it to my friends, my kind of people, or those I like. The meaning of the text is obvious, unambiguous, and explicit.[4]

---

3. Rom. 14:1–15:7.
4. Luke 10:25–37.

But how far am I supposed to take it? If I hear about a need on the local news, am I supposed to rush out and help? Am I responsible for the plight of those who are brought to my attention by slick fundraising campaigns and media blitzes? Am I supposed to take the initiative and hunt for people in need? Does my neighbor include everyone in the world, or was Jesus perhaps just talking about those I come across in the course of my normal daily activities?

These are tough questions. We'll all have slightly different answers. And in many cases, we feel strongly about them. That's what makes a text like this particularly prone to a spirit of legalism. It's easy for my answers to become the answers by which I judge everyone else.

But no matter how strong my personal convictions may be, at the end of the day, my own application of the text is just that — *my own* application. To turn it into anything else undercuts freedom in Christ. It arrogantly usurps the authority of the Holy Spirit. It points me down a path to the place where Pharisees, both ancient and accidental, have long dwelt — the land of legalism.

Perhaps that's why the apostle Paul told the quarrelling Romans, "So whatever you believe about these things keep between yourself and God." Ultimately, we'll have to figure these things out on our own, wrestling with the text and listening to the Spirit's leading. Otherwise freedom in Christ becomes nothing but an empty buzzword, cast aside and replaced by a harsh one-size-fits-all spirituality.[5]

---

5. Rom. 14:2–4, 22.

CHAPTER 12

THE DEATH OF MERCY

The Darkest and Most Dangerous Side of Legalism

The absolute worst thing about legalism is what it does to mercy. It casts it aside, then walks away. It leaves people who need mercy most to fend for themselves and castigates those who offer mercy as spiritual compromisers who water down the gospel.

That's because legalists have always viewed the application of mercy as selling out. They love the *idea* of mercy, but they want to limit when it's offered and whom it's offered to. Nothing illustrates this selectivity better than Jesus' running battle with the Pharisees over the Sabbath. Every time he healed somebody on the Sabbath, it drove them nuts.

THE FIGHT JESUS LOVED TO PICK

The rules surrounding the Sabbath were some of Jesus' favorite rules to break. So much so that he sometimes deliberately picked a fight by not only healing on the Sabbath but also making a big show of it.[1]

---

1. Mark 3:1–5. One time, before healing a man with a shriveled hand, Jesus asked him to stand up in front of everyone just so the Pharisees would see what he was doing. They were so upset, they began to plot how to kill Jesus.

The fourth commandment forbade working on the Sabbath.[2] But *work* is a nebulous term, open to differing interpretations. So the religious scholars took it upon themselves to help God out and define it precisely. They decreed what was work and what wasn't, how far you could walk, what you could carry, whom you could help, and what things had to wait until the next day.

For instance, they decided that if your animal fell into a pit, you could lift it out to save its life. That wasn't work. However, practicing medicine was work. So if your friend was sick, you couldn't provide medication or do anything to make him better (including a miraculous healing). That had to wait until the Sabbath was over.

Why the Pharisees Deserve a Break

With the 20/20 hindsight of history, it's easy to ridicule and blast the Pharisees for their hard-hearted rigidity. But I wonder whose side I would have been on had I been a part of the crowd, without the advantage of knowing the end of the story.

It's a sobering question, because if I'm honest, the Pharisees' values, their logic, and the rationale they used in arguing with Jesus were not much different than my own — or that of any of us who are deeply committed to God, his glory, and the Bible.

First, they were attempting to be meticulously obedient to Scripture. They weren't looking for loopholes or the easy way out. They were striving to live up to the highest possible standard. If that meant some pain and suffering along the way (for them or for others), so be it. This was a small price to pay for the pursuit of righteousness.

Second, their rules weren't nearly as arbitrary as they might seem to us today. The Pharisees didn't just make them up. The rules were based on the rigorous study of Scripture. They followed countless hours of debate. They were backed by carefully nuanced logic. No one could accuse the Pharisees of taking Scripture lightly or having a cavalier attitude toward the things of God.

---

2. Exod. 20:8–11.

Third, none of the people Jesus healed on a Sabbath were in grave danger. All of them could have waited until sundown — easily. So why not wait? From a Pharisee's perspective, it must have appeared that Jesus was putting the immediate needs of humankind above faithful adherence to Scripture and the fear of God.

MERCY FOR EVERYONE — EVEN PEOPLE WHO "DON'T DESERVE IT"

Jesus didn't care. He wouldn't listen to their logic. He wouldn't postpone his mercy to fit their timetable. Instead he kept picking fights to prove a point: in the kingdom of God, mercy trumps sacrifice. Always.[3]

Here's something noteworthy that most people miss. Jesus didn't apply his mercy just to people in dire straits. He applied it everywhere, to everyone, lavishly. The needs of the blind, lame, and disfigured were more important than rigid sacrificial adherence to Sabbath laws. But so were the needs of some friends who were merely hungry.

One day when his disciples were walking through a grain field on the Sabbath, they plucked some heads of grain, husked them, and ate them. This freaked out the Pharisees. The scriptural prohibition against working on the Sabbath specifically forbade harvesting.[4] Even though it was just a simple act of grabbing a stalk, rubbing off its husks, and eating what was inside, it was clearly a form of harvesting.

The Pharisees expected Jesus to immediately put a stop to this. But he did nothing. This upset them all the more. From their perspective, the hunger of the disciples was no excuse to justify a clear violation of the Sabbath law. All they had to do was wait a few hours. They weren't going to starve. Once the Sabbath was over, they could eat all they wanted.

Frankly, I think their argument makes sense. I get where they were coming from. Had I been there, I probably would have

---

3. Hos. 6:6; Matt. 9:13.
4. Exod. 34:21.

agreed with them. Bet you would have too. There's just one problem. Jesus didn't agree with them.[5]

A LESSON FROM DAVID'S LIFE

He shot down their objections with a story from the life of one of their favorite heroes, King David. Before David became king, he and his men were on the run, hotly pursued by King Saul. One day, hungry and exhausted, they entered the house of God and asked for food. Unfortunately, the only thing the priest had was some of the showbread—the special bread that was baked weekly and consecrated to God. Only the priest and his family members were allowed to eat it.

Since David and his men were famished, there were only two options. They could eat the forbidden showbread, or they would collapse from hunger, get caught, and be killed. So they ate the showbread and went on their way.[6]

What they did was clearly forbidden. There is no way to twist the story to make it otherwise, though lots of people have tried to do so. It was a clear violation of the regulations spelled out in Leviticus.[7] Yet for Jesus, it was the perfect example of God's priorities and the importance of always putting mercy above a harsh and rigid sacrificial observance of the Law.

Jesus made it clear that the Pharisees had it backward (as legalists always do). Man wasn't made for the Sabbath. The Sabbath was made for man. It was a gift to make people's lives better, a guaranteed day of rest even during the hectic days of planting and harvest. The Sabbath was never meant to be a test to see how much people were willing to give up for God.

MERCY WITHOUT LIMITS

What's remarkable (and too often ignored by the legalists among us) is that Jesus didn't limit the lesson of David and the showbread to crisis situations. He used it to defend his disciples picking and

---

5. Mark 2:23–28.
6. 1 Sam. 21:1–6.
7. Lev. 22:10–11.

eating grain on the Sabbath to satisfy their passing hunger rather than waiting a few hours until sundown.

But that was the point. Mercy really is more important than sacrifice. It's not a cliché. It's a reality. It's a kingdom principle. It's what God wants. It's to be applied everywhere. Even if it drives the religious elite crazy.

It's here that we see most clearly the difference between the mercy of Jesus and the "mercy" of the modern-day legalist. Legalists offer mercy. But the mercy they offer has limits. They have plenty of mercy for those overseas, mercy for those who face tough odds, mercy for those who don't yet know Jesus.

But there's very little mercy for struggling brothers and sisters in Christ. There's not much sympathy for people who are weak and faltering. For those folks, there's nothing but a harsh rebuke and stinging exhortations to catch up with the rest of us, often with a disclaimer that they're probably not even real Christians anyway.

Unfortunately, the more zealous and passionate we become, the easier it is to fall into the trap of harsh legalism. We can become so focused on the so-called hard sayings of Jesus that we miss the incredible compassion and mercy he showed to the weakest and most vulnerable of his flock.

To both ancient and accidental Pharisees, mercy is a scary thing to offer other disciples. We fear that they might take advantage of it or see it as permission to live in halfhearted obedience.

Not so with Jesus.

To people who fail, turn away, or sit on the fence because they are too afraid to jump in or are not yet fully convinced, Jesus continues to offer his extravagant mercy, a helping hand, and another chance. It isn't weakness. It's not compromise. It's mercy: excessive, undeserved, and generous.

Yet when we fall prey to legalism, this kind of mercy gets shoved aside as weakness and compromise. We no longer have any room for doubters, deniers, secret disciples, ladder climbers, or anyone else who doesn't get it or can't keep up at the front of the line. We want a pure church. So we shoo them away.

Thankfully for many of us, Jesus takes a different route.

Discussion Questions for Part 4

Legalism

1. "Litmus test Christianity" is a dangerous type of legalism that can cause us to write off other genuine Christians as bogus Christians. It's an easy trap to fall into.

   a. Do you find yourself naturally drawn toward the clarifying lines of "litmus test Christianity" or repelled by them? If so, why do you think that is?

   b. Which, if any, of the tribes listed in chapter 10 would you fit best in? Are there any other litmus tests that you or your tribe might be prone to use? If so, list them.

2. In part 4 we looked at both "old-school legalism" and "new-school legalism." Which of the two do you think you or your church are most tempted to fall into? Why? What are some of the dangers that come with it?

3. The Pharisees of old added to the Scriptures in an attempt to help God out. Looking back over your Christian journey, have you come across examples of people:

   a. Adding to Scripture? And if so, how so?

    b. Turning implications into commands (making the personal application of a passage a universal rule for everyone)? Again, what are some examples?

4. What lessons can we take away from the "diet wars" and the "Sabbath wars" of the New Testament days?

    a. What are some present-day equivalents of the New Testament diet wars and Sabbath wars?

    b. How might Paul's instructions to the Romans apply to these modern-day issues?

5. Accidental Pharisees often are driven by the fear that showing too much mercy will lead to compromise and half-hearted obedience. But the fact is that we all tend to treat some sins as less deserving of mercy than others. Why do you think that is? And which ones do you have the hardest time offering mercy to?

PART 5

IDOLIZING THE PAST

When Idealism Distorts Reality

CHAPTER 13

THE PROBLEM WITH ROSE-COLORED MEMORIES

Why These Might Be the Good Old Days

Have you noticed that most of us tend to view the past through rose-colored glasses? Whether it's an old boyfriend or girlfriend, memories of our high school glory days, the moral fiber of previous generations, or our images of the early church, we're inclined to remember things as far better than they were.

In one sense, this is a good thing. Who wants to spend time dwelling on the hurts and injustices of the past? I'd rather remember the good times than focus on the bad. I'm thankful that the pain of yesterday is often hard to recall.

But our rose-colored memories can also have a detrimental effect. They can blind us to the beauties of the present. They can distort reality. They can leave us with an unholy dissatisfaction, where every glass is half empty and our dreams of the future are nothing but a longing for a nonexistent past.

I've seen romanticized memories destroy marriages. Bored husbands and wives reconnect with an old flame on Facebook or at a high school reunion. After comparing the slog of the present with an idealized memory of the past, they cast off the drudgery of today to reclaim the glories of yesterday. Unfortunately, they always seem to forget *why* the old relationship ended in the first place. But it usually doesn't take long for them to remember. And by then it's too late. They're caught in a back-to-the-future nightmare.

I've also watched the relentless pursuit of a romanticized past lead people to displace their families, sidetrack their careers, and squander their finances. I've seen it tear apart churches, obliterate contentment, and destroy legacies. Perhaps that's why the author of Ecclesiastes wrote, "Do not say, 'Why were the old days better than these?' For it is not wise to ask such questions."[1]

He knew what we so quickly forget: These are the good old days. Or they will be before long.

THE BLESSING AND CURSE OF IDEALISM

I'm not sure why this is true, but passionate faith is often coupled with a zealous idealism and a romanticized view of the past.

On the one hand, our idealism can be a blessing. A healthy dose of idealism drives us to change things. It refuses to fatalistically settle and accept the status quo. It powers the dogged pursuit of what could be and *should* be. Idealism provides the fuel that turns our crazy dreams into reality.

But on the other hand, idealism can also be a curse. If it flows out of an inaccurate and overly romanticized view of the past, it can lead to a desperate longing for what never was and a deep frustration with whatever is.

Perhaps you have some friends who never enjoy the present because they're so sure everything used to be better. They're like

---

1. Ecc. 7:10.

greyhounds on the racetrack, chasing a stuffed rabbit they'll never catch. Their endless pursuit of the perfect marriage, the flawless family, the ideal career, or the perfect church leaves them perpetually unsatisfied.

Yet perpetual discontent is not the worst thing that idealism's rose-colored memories produce. There is something far worse. It's cynicism, the negative and harsh critique of everything and everyone. Cynicism is idealism on steroids. It has an eagle's eye for what is wrong and a bat's blindness for what's praiseworthy. The religious leaders of Jesus' day were classic cynics. They had a long history of killing the prophets and then later erecting monuments in their name.[2]

Today's spiritual elite are no different. They too tend to be cynical. They don't kill anyone, but they're masters at finding fault, especially with their three favorite whipping boys — the church, its leaders, and current culture. If you read or hear any of their critiques, it's hard not to become depressed or angry at the church and the world we live in.

But before you lose all hope for the future, you might want to remember two things that today's negative pundits never seem to bring up. First, they fail to mention that the church, its leaders, and culture have been the target of scathing critiques for centuries. It's nothing new. Second, they seem to forget that *everything* has been screwed up since Genesis 3.

So let's take a brief look at the church, its leaders, and culture to see if things are really as bad as they've been made out to be and if yesterday was really as great as everyone says it was.

THE CHURCH

There's no question that today's church is far from perfect. When we compare it with the past, especially the early church we read about in the New Testament, it can seem like there isn't much to praise.

But the church has always been messed up. You can find plenty of contemporary critics of the church from fifty years, one

---

2. Luke 11:47–51.

hundred years, or even five hundred years ago that deride the church of their day, equating it with the churches in Laodicea and Ephesus—the two miserable churches that Jesus denounced in the book of Revelation.[3]

For instance, five hundred years ago the church appeared to be on life support. The Scriptures had become buried beneath so many layers of tradition and ritual that no one in the pews knew what they actually said. The church was so obsessed with money that some of its leaders were offering forgiveness and a free pass into heaven in exchange for a healthy donation. Those were definitely not the good old days.

One hundred years ago a tsunami of liberalism swept over seminaries and over many of the most prestigious pulpits in the land. Many of the largest and most influential ministry platforms were filled by pastors and theologians who denied the supernatural, rejected the fundamentals of the faith, and questioned the reliability of the Bible. They proclaimed a truncated gospel designed to fit better with modern sensibilities. Again, that hardly sounds like the good old days. I don't think any of us would want to go back.

And it was just fifty years ago that scholars bemoaned the cultural irrelevance of the church. Many wondered if the local church still had a future. *Time* magazine posed the question on its cover: "Is God Dead?"[4] Experts predicted the end of propositional truth, the need for dialogues instead of preaching, and the unwillingness of anyone to put up with a sermon longer than fifteen or twenty minutes.

But they were wrong. The local church did have a future despite all of its warts and failings. And we shouldn't be surprised. Jesus said something about building his church and the gates of hell not being able to hold it back.[5]

Throughout history, every time the church has seemed primed

---

3. Revelation 2:1–5 and 3:14–16 describe a church that had lost its first love and a church that was lukewarm, both in danger of facing God's immediate judgment.

4. *Time* (April 8, 1966).

5. Matt. 16:18.

for certain demise, God has had something up his sleeve. Five hundred years ago it was the Reformation. One hundred years ago it was the rise of the Bible school movement and evangelicalism. Fifty years ago it was the Jesus Movement. I'm pretty sure he's got a plan for today. Two thousand years of church history and the clear promise of the one who founded the church give me lots of hope.

CHURCH LEADERS

There is no question that today's pastors and spiritual leaders are also far from perfect. You don't have to dig too deep to find prominent examples of ego, greed, turf battles, doctrinal error, and sin. Both nationally known superstars and anonymous leaders toiling in the trenches struggle with the lust of the flesh, the lust of the eyes, and the pride of life.[6]

But once again, this is nothing new. God has always drawn straight lines with crooked sticks. Abraham was a liar, Moses a murderer, David an adulterer, and Peter a denier.

But a strange thing happens with the passage of time. The farther removed we get from the stick, the more likely we are to credit the stick (rather than the divine artist) as the reason for the straight line. And the closer we are to a crooked stick, the harder it is for us to see the straight line being drawn.

Pastors and ministry leaders who have a large following or a significant kingdom impact are carefully scrutinized. Their slightest flaws or failings are put under the microscope and closely examined. Woe to the public figure who misspeaks, missteps, believes or teaches a falsehood, or is exposed as a sinner. The blogosphere lights up. Even the slightest failures go viral.

At least until these people die. Then everything changes. With the passage of time, we begin to magnify the good and forget the bad. Pretty soon you can earn a PhD studying their life and ministry. Those who were loudly criticized while they lived will have seminaries, denominations, and conference grounds named after them decades after they die. It's our way of building monuments.

---

6. 1 John 2:16.

This pattern goes all the way back to the church fathers. We revere them. But a few held theological views that would get them kicked out of our churches. If they were alive today, they wouldn't be allowed to teach a junior high Sunday school class. But in their day, God allowed them to lead his church.

Fast-forward a millennium to someone like John Calvin. Calvin was a prolific writer and a profound theologian. But he also allowed his followers to torture and kill one of his opponents, burning him at the stake for denying the Trinity and strongly opposing infant baptism. No matter how you slice it, that's hard to defend, justify, or explain away. Yet Calvin remains one of the most quoted and admired theologians of our day.

Or take a closer look at Martin Luther. His anti-Semitic writings are embarrassing. Yet most Protestants wouldn't hesitate to trace their roots back to the ninety-five theses he nailed to the Wittenberg door. Without Luther's courage and his commitment to the authority of Scripture alone, the church might still be selling indulgences.

Or consider men like John Wesley, A. W. Tozer, or Bob Pierce (the founder of World Vision). All of them had horrendous marriages. They tragically and sinfully neglected their families in the pursuit of ministry. Yet they remain heroes of the faith. The good they accomplished is widely honored, while their failures have long been forgotten.

To be clear, all of these men were powerfully used by God. They accomplished great things. But they were also deeply flawed—sinners saved by grace. And the same is true of the current crop of leaders whom God is using today. They are broken. They are sinners. They make mistakes—sometimes big mistakes. Yet God continues to use them in his grace. He's still drawing straight lines with crooked sticks. Odds are that he'll continue to do so until Jesus comes back.

CULTURE

The third whipping boy that the pundits love to disparage is the culture of our day. Admittedly, its current godless trajectory is alarming. It's natural to wonder what might come next. Even worse, the core values of our culture seem to have crept into the church.

But again, is this all that new? Hasn't this been happening for two thousand years? Isn't that why the apostle Paul had to tell the Christians in Rome to *stop* conforming to the pattern of this world and to be transformed by the renewing of their minds so that they could experience the good, pleasing, and perfect will of God?[7]

The naysayers fall into two traps. They project the future as if culture moves in a straight line, and they view the past through an inaccurate and romanticized lens.

For instance, baby boomers were projected to remain antiauthoritarian, pot-smoking, anarchist. No one would have pegged them for SUVs, minivans, and Tommy Bahama shirts. Gen Xers were pegged as slackers who would never get a real job. But things changed quickly when dot-com options were dangled in front of them. And millennials were supposed to usher in a civic-minded, industrious society of do-gooders. That is, when they weren't pale-skinned Quake addicts, wannabe gangsta rappers, or hyped-up on ecstasy.

Or consider the so-called Greatest Generation. It was actually assailed in the press and criticized by its elders as the Lost Generation.[8] Newspaper headlines, magazine covers, and government studies lamented a generation without a thought for social responsibility, out for what they could get. The American Youth Commission published a report that said 75 percent of one hundred thousand young men tested were suffering from some health

---

7. Rom. 12:2.

8. Tom Brokaw's bestseller *The Greatest Generation* lauded the youth of the 1930s, who toiled through the Great Depression, won World War II, and then supplied three decades of statesmanship and stability as "the greatest generation any society has ever produced." But in 1939, Maxine Johnson traveled ten thousand miles studying the "Lost Generation," a term that became the title of her book about confused, disillusioned, disenchanted youth in a state "rapidly approaching a psychosis."

defect induced by mental anxiety. No one appears to have guessed that this Lost Generation would one day be called the Greatest Generation.[9]

The same goes for the naysayers' romanticized memories of the past. Granted, if you were a white suburbanite, there was a lot to like in the 1950s. But if you were a black man living in Birmingham, a Jew trying to join the LA Country Club, or a Japanese American family trying to recover from a forced stint in an internment camp, those weren't the good old days — or so innocent, or biblically aligned.

All of this gives me great pause. It tempers my tendency to catastrophize the future. It makes me slow to join the chorus of people who claim the sky is falling. It gives me hope that perhaps the imperfect church, its leaders, and the culture of my day may one day be looked back upon with the fondness reserved for the good old days.

9. Mike Males, "For Adults, 'Today's Youth' Are Always the Worst," *LA Times* (November 21, 1999).

CHAPTER 14

LEARNING FROM THE PAST WITHOUT IDOLIZING THE PAST

An Honest Look at the New Testament Church

It has been said that people who don't learn from the past are doomed to repeat the past. It's true. That's why, as Christians, we need to learn all we can from the New Testament church. What did they do right? Where did they goof up? What brought God's blessings? What brought his disapproval?

But to learn from the past, we have to have an accurate picture of the past. Unfortunately, many of us have an image of the New Testament church that has little to do with reality. We picture it filled with on-fire, turn-the-world-upside-down supersaints charging the hill for Jesus. But that's not how it was.

The early church was messed up, just like today's church. It was filled with sinners—forgiven, but sinners nonetheless. To learn from them, we have to cut through the fog of clichés, assumptions, and favorite verses to drill down to the facts.

That's not always easy. But it's important.

Like many Christians, I've long been fascinated by the New Testament church. I came to Christ late in my high school years and immediately felt a call toward ministry. In the book of Acts, I found a description of a church that stirred my heart. It seemed to be far different from anything I'd ever experienced—dynamic, pure, completely sold out.

So once I became a pastor, the early church as described in Acts (especially Acts 2) became my template for ministry. I used the description of its gatherings, priorities, and growth as the metric by which to evaluate our progress toward becoming a New Testament church.

But then a strange thing happened. As I read the texts more closely, I began to see a number of things I'd never noticed before. I began to wonder if the passages that I'd always seen as *prescriptions* of what should be were merely *descriptions* of what once was, and not very flattering descriptions at that.

Let's see what I mean.

THE CHURCH IN JERUSALEM

The most famous and oft-quoted verses describing the early church in Jerusalem are found in Acts 2:42–47. Here's what they say.

> They devoted themselves to the apostles' teaching and to fellowship, to the breaking of bread and to prayer. Everyone was filled with awe at the many wonders and signs performed by the apostles. All the believers were together and had everything in common. They sold property and possessions to give to anyone who had need. Every day they continued to meet together in the temple courts. They broke bread in their homes and ate together with glad and sincere hearts, praising God and enjoying the favor of all the people. And the Lord added to their number daily those who were being saved.

But here's what I thought the passage said. The strikethroughs represent the phrases that I (and most of the folks in my tribe) never seemed to notice.

> They devoted themselves to the apostles' teaching and to fellowship, to the breaking of bread and to prayer. Everyone was filled with awe ~~at the many wonders and signs performed by the apostles~~. All the believers were together ~~and had everything in common~~. They sold property and possessions to give to anyone who had need. ~~Every day~~ they continued to meet together ~~in the temple courts~~. They broke bread in their homes and ate together with glad and sincere hearts, praising God and enjoying the favor of all the people. And the Lord added to their number daily those who were being saved.

If this passage is a recipe for a God-pleasing church, we were leaving out some key ingredients. But we weren't alone. Every tribe does the same thing. The only difference is what we choose to highlight and what we decide to ignore.

For instance, everybody loves the idea of thousands coming to Christ and being baptized. Everyone embraces the importance of the apostles' teaching, fellowship, breaking of bread, and prayer. We all think it's a great thing to praise God and enjoy favor in the eyes of the people.

But my Pentecostal brothers and sisters always raise a concern. They want to know why the rest of us ignore the part about the apostles performing many signs and wonders. They think that's the reason why everyone was filled with awe. After all, as they like to point out, that is what the text says.

Then there are my friends on the far left (and a few old hippies who used to live in a commune). They have a different complaint. They want to know why everybody ignores the part about *everyone* having *everything* in common. For them, that's the game changer. They think that's what made the early church a family. But my Republican friends aren't so sure. They think it's just a figure of speech.

I have still other friends who point to the verse that talks about selling property and possessions to give to anyone in need. They want to know why that's so rare in our churches today. But these same folks never seem to notice the verse *before* their favorite verse. The one that says everyone had everything in common. On that point, they tend to agree with the Republicans that it's just a figure of speech.

Finally, there is something in this passage that no one wants to emulate. It's the idea of meeting *every day*, especially if that means meeting in Jerusalem, in the temple courts. Somehow that never makes it into anyone's prescription for a New Testament church.

All this makes it hard to justify using the church in Jerusalem as a template for the church of today. If we're honest with the text, it's more of a description than a prescription. But there's still more to the story. If we look carefully, we'll discover that the church in Jerusalem is also a template we wouldn't want to follow if we could. For starters, they ignored the Great Commission.[1]

Ignoring the Great Commission

After his resurrection, Jesus told everyone to wait in Jerusalem until they received the promised Holy Spirit. When the Spirit came, they would be empowered to go into Judea, Samaria, and to the ends of the earth sharing the good news and making disciples. But until then they had to wait.[2]

But here's the sad part. When the Spirit came, they didn't go. Instead they hunkered down in a holy huddle. It wasn't until God sent a great persecution that they finally left the city. Only then did they scatter throughout Judea and Samaria preaching the good news as they had been commanded to do.[3]

It's easy to understand why they stayed. The fellowship must have been amazing, and the signs and wonders mind-blowing. On top of that, they expected Jesus to return any day, because when he ascended into heaven, two angels had appeared to them, saying he would come back in the same manner they had seen him go.[4]

---

1. Matt. 28:18–20.
2. Luke 24:46–49; Acts 1:4–8.
3. Acts 8:1–4.
4. Acts 1:10–11.

They assumed it would be soon and it would take place right there in Jerusalem. So they stayed.

Running out of Money

Their decision to hang around and wait for Jesus' return not only caused them to ignore the Great Commission; it also caused them to run out of money.

Remember that the city was swelled with swarms of pilgrims on the day of Pentecost. People who became believers that day would have likely stayed in order to be there when Jesus came back. It doesn't make much sense to return home if you're convinced that the Messiah is coming back any day.

But they would have also quickly run out of funds. There were no ATMs, credit cards, or checking accounts. Once they used up the money they'd brought with them, they had only two options: head back home or depend on the hospitality and generosity of others.

For those who lived in Jerusalem, it was a no-brainer. In a culture where hospitality was one of the highest values, it made perfect sense to sell off properties and possessions so that everyone could stay around until Jesus came back.

I've often wondered what part this played in creating the poverty that later engulfed the Jerusalem church. They became so impoverished that the apostle Paul collected a special offering from all of his Gentile churches for the poor saints in Jerusalem.[5]

I also wonder if this explains why the New Testament letters never command or even encourage the same kind of selling of property and possessions (or the pooling of resources) that we find described in the early days of the Jerusalem church.

I don't know. No one can say for sure. But it sure does make me wonder.

The Gentile Problem

There was another area where the Jerusalem church failed to get it right. They had a little problem with Gentiles. They weren't welcome. They wanted to keep everything kosher.

---

5. 2 Corinthians 8–9 includes Paul's instructions for this special offering.

Don't miss this. It's a big deal. It was a major spiritual failing. There's no way to sugarcoat it. The church in Jerusalem was racist.

Even the apostle Peter was unwilling to share the gospel with a Gentile. God had to send him a special vision, and he had to repeat it three times. Then after it became clear that a Gentile named Cornelius had indeed been saved and filled with the Holy Spirit, Peter had to call a special meeting before everyone else would accept it. And even then, many in the Jerusalem church continued to insist that Gentiles could be saved (and welcomed) only if they adopted Jewish laws and customs.[6]

My bet is that most of you reading this are Gentiles. It's rather sobering to realize that the church that many of us want to model ourselves after wouldn't have welcomed us.

None of this is meant to say that the early church in Jerusalem was a shameful failure. It was an incredible miracle. But it was a miracle of grace and mercy. It was a church filled with forgiven sinners who struggled with the same kinds of things we still struggle with today. And that gives me hope, not only for today's church but also for the future.

NEW TESTAMENT LEADERS

By the way, it's not just the church in Jerusalem that wasn't all it's cracked up to be. The same holds true for the leaders in the early church. They were also far from perfect.

For instance, Peter was a hypocrite. While he's famous for his ups and downs, his foot-in-mouth disease, and the three times he denied knowing Jesus, all of that took place before he saw the resurrected Lord and was filled with the Spirit, so most people think that after that, everything was different. But it wasn't.

One time while he was in the town of Antioch, a group of legalists and Judaizers came down from Jerusalem to force the Gentiles to follow Jewish religious laws. Peter gave in to their pressure and

---

6. Acts 10:1–11:18 and 15:1–21 record Peter's reluctance, Cornelius's salvation, and the debates that followed regarding the appropriateness of including Gentiles.

pretended to support a cause he knew was wrong. It was hypocritical, weak-kneed, and disingenuous. It led others astray. So much so that the apostle Paul had to publically rebuke him for it.[7]

But then again, the apostle Paul had his own issues.

To begin with, he had an immense struggle with pride. His bent toward arrogance was so strong that God sent a "thorn in the flesh," a messenger of Satan, to torment him and keep him from becoming conceited. Apparently, it was the only way to keep him from flaming out.[8]

Then there was his mercy-deprived response to John Mark. John Mark had gone with Paul and Barnabas on a mission trip. When things got tough, he chickened out and went back home. When it was time to go on another trip, Barnabas wanted to give John Mark a second chance. But Paul refused. He wouldn't budge. It became such a big issue that Paul and Barnabas split over it. As far as we know, they never worked together again.[9]

It's hard to believe, but the self-described chief of sinners, the poster child for God's unmerited grace and mercy, refused to give John Mark a second chance. And time seems to have proved Paul wrong, because God chose John Mark to write the gospel of Mark, which means that God considered him worthy to write part of the Bible, but Paul didn't think he was worthy to go on a short-term mission trip. Go figure.

But Peter and Paul weren't the only ones with feet of clay. The early church was filled with leaders who were less than stellar. Timothy was timid. Demas bailed out because he loved the world. Diotrephes was a little dictator, so intent on being first that he wouldn't allow the apostle John to visit his congregation. And at one point, the apostle Paul looked around and couldn't think of anyone other than Timothy who would put the interests of Christ above his own personal interest.[10]

---

7. Gal. 2:11–14.

8. 2 Cor. 12:7–10.

9. Acts 15:36–41.

10. 1 Tim. 4:12; 2 Tim. 1:7 (Timothy); 2 Tim. 4:10 (Demas); 3 John 9–10 (Diotrephes); Phil. 2:19–22.

All of this puts a new perspective on our current crop of leaders. Maybe they aren't so bad after all. Maybe God will continue to draw straight lines with crooked sticks, just like he did in the first century.

THE OTHER NEW TESTAMENT CHURCHES

As long as we are being brutally honest about the New Testament church and its leaders, we need to note one more thing. The apostle Paul planted some pretty lame churches. That's why he had to write all those letters.

The church in Galatia was quickly enamored with a different gospel. It happened so quickly that Paul was astonished. It was so off base that they were in danger of being separated from Christ. Paul had to rebuke them sharply, reminding them that if salvation could be found in religious traditions and laws, then Christ died needlessly.[11]

Then there was the church in Ephesus. It looked great on the surface, but it was rotting on the inside. Sure, it was doctrinally sound, filled with dedicated, hardworking people who persevered in the face of hardship, but the *agape* love they started out with had faded away to the point that Jesus warned them that he would remove his presence if they didn't hurry up and repent.[12]

The church in Philippi was filled with generous people. They comprised Paul's primary donor base. His gratitude for their support was the catalyst for the book of Philippians. But they were also torn apart by a bitter church fight between two women, Euodia and Syntyche. Paul had to plead with them to get along and asked everyone else to help them work it out.[13]

Or consider his strange instructions to Timothy and Titus. When Paul told them how to pick leaders in the church, he

---

11. Gal. 1–6.
12. Eph. 1–6.
13. Phil. 1–4.

advised them to avoid the town drunk, along with anyone with a violent temper, an argumentative spirit, or a history of dishonest business dealings or marital unfaithfulness.[14]

That seems rather odd. Even the sickest churches I know don't have to be told to keep those kinds of people out of leadership. But apparently the early church was so raw that Paul thought Timothy and Titus needed to be told. It's one more window into what the early church was really like.

As for the Corinthians, well, let's just say that they were so spiritually dysfunctional that Paul had to write two letters to them — and long letters at that. They had divided into different camps based on their favorite teachers and leaders. They ignored blatant sin in the name of tolerance. They sued one another. They continued to visit temple prostitutes. They argued about dietary laws. Their public meetings were extremely contentious, producing more harm than good. Their Communion services were so whacked-out that some folks became ill and weak, and a few even died. They had potlucks where no one shared, and people who had nothing went home humiliated. They emphasized the gifts of the Spirit but ignored the love that flows from the Spirit. And some of them were teaching that there was no resurrection from the dead. And those are just the problems Paul addressed in his first letter![15]

All of this helps to explain why I consider our idolization of the New Testament church to be a rose-colored memory. It's why I always ask people who deride the present-day church and long for a return to the New Testament church, "Have you actually read the New Testament?"

The early church teaches us many lessons. But there are as many lessons about what *not* to do as lessons about what to do. And one of the most important things we can learn from the failings of the early church is the danger of idolizing the past to the point of losing hope and perspective in the present.

---

14. 1 Tim. 3:1–12; Titus 1:5–9.
15. 1 Cor. 1–16.

God has always drawn straight lines with crooked sticks. He has always used the weak to show off his strength. He has always chosen the undeserving to demonstrate his grace. We should not be surprised if he continues to do the same thing today.

CHAPTER 15

SPEAKING THE TRUTH IN LOVE

Confronting the Present without Lionizing the Past

So there you have it. Sometimes you have to blast before you build. But the blasting is done. Hopefully, I've made my case. The good old days weren't always so great. The sins and failings of today's church and disciples, though significant, are nothing new. They won't keep Jesus from continuing to build his church just as he promised.

Yet merely breaking the stranglehold of an inaccurate and romanticized view of the past doesn't do much to fix the problems of today. It merely puts them in perspective. To correct them, we have to do more.

So how should we go about it? How can we critique, confront, and rebuke the failings of today's church and struggling disciples in a way that provokes genuine repentance and change?

There is no better model than the apostle Paul's two letters to the Corinthian church. The Corinthians were as off base as you can get. Still, Paul met all of their issues head-on. He didn't pull any punches. He critiqued and rebuked everything that was out of line. Yet he did so without a trace of the disgust and caustic cynicism that is so common today among those of us who feel called to set the church and God's people straight.

How did he do it? And what did he do?

FIND THE GOOD AND PRAISE IT

The first thing to notice about Paul's rebuke of the Corinthian church is the way he starts out. He begins with praise. Not contempt. Not critique. Not a scolding. Though there was plenty to rant about.

He finds the good and praises it, sincerely and genuinely. He's not blowing smoke. He's not setting them up. He is writing Scripture; his words reflect the heart and viewpoint of God!

He begins by reminding them of who they are in Christ, even though they aren't living like it. He points out that they have been set apart, called to be holy. He affirms that they are enriched in speech and knowledge, that they don't lack any spiritual gift, and that they are eagerly awaiting the return of Jesus. He also assures them that despite their many sins and failings, they will be kept firm to the end, found blameless on the day of the Lord.[1]

He did all that in the first nine verses!

Contrast that with how we tend to address the sins and failings of the church today.

To begin with, most of our stinging rebukes have not a word of praise. I've never heard a conference speaker, read a book, or sat with friends who began their critique of our Corinth-like churches with a list of praiseworthy traits. Instead we go right for the jugular. We start with the bad and move on to the horrible. Our tone can be scornful as we ridicule, mock, and question the salvation of everyone who's at the back of the line.

Second, we seldom speak directly to those in need of correction. I find it interesting that the apostle Paul never wrote any letters that criticized *other* churches. Instead all of his corrective

---

1. 1 Cor. 1:1–9.

letters were written to the church needing the critique. Most of our criticisms are voiced to one another about someone else. From the pages of a book, from the pulpit, or from the stage of a packed-out conference (attended primarily by other leaders), we fire away at the weak, the struggling, and the Corinth-like churches in a way that does nothing to help them change but does plenty to puff us up with an abundance of self-congratulatory pride.

Faced with the sins and carnality of the Corinthians, Paul addressed them differently. He didn't merely talk about them to others. He wrote to them directly. He also treated them as fellow saints with whom God was not yet finished. He sincerely praised what the Lord had started, before forcefully dealing with the many things that still needed work. In essence, he followed the same advice he gave the Philippians when they were worried and concerned. He focused on what was admirable, excellent, and praiseworthy.[2] Then he spoke the truth in love.

SPEAK THE TRUTH IN LOVE

The longer I live, the more I recognize the importance of a proper attitude and motivation when confronting the sins and failings of others.

Paul wrote with a broken heart. He felt great distress. He shed many tears. He loved the Corinthians as if they were his own children.[3] Yet many of the harsh critics that I hear and read today seem to have far more disgust than tears. I'd never characterize them as compassionate or loving. Their critiques feel more like a venting of pent-up frustrations than a brokenhearted call to repentance. These people don't appear to love the weak. They're angry at the weak.

Again, contrast that to Paul's attitude toward the Corinthians. Despite their many sins and hard-hearted ways, he did more than just "love them in the Lord." He actually liked them. He was proud of them. He even bragged on them to others. He said so himself. All of which I find mind-boggling in light of the mess he

---

2. Phil. 4:8.
3. 1 Cor. 4:14; 2 Cor. 2:4; 6:13.

feared he would find when he showed up.[4] "I am afraid that when I come," he wrote, "I may not find you as I want you to be, and you may not find me as you want me to be. I fear that there may be discord, jealousy, fits of rage, selfish ambition, slander, gossip, arrogance and disorder. I am afraid that when I come again my God will humble me before you, and I will be grieved over many who have sinned earlier and have not repented of the impurity, sexual sin and debauchery in which they have indulged."[5]

There will never be a shortage of unhealthy Christians and unhealthy churches. The only place they'll ever be in short supply is in our romanticized images of the past. And therein lies the three great temptations of idolizing the past.

The first is to think that the sins and failings of today are something new and rare. Nothing could be farther from the truth. It's a lie. People who believe it become despairing and cynical, blind to what God is doing in the present, while building monuments to what he did in the past.

The second is to lash out in anger and disgust. Like James and John (whom Jesus nicknamed the Sons of Thunder), we can wish for fire from heaven upon those who reject Jesus. But Jesus didn't rebuke the Samaritans who rejected him; he rebuked James and John for their anger and harsh response.[6]

The third is to attempt to help out Jesus by yanking out all the weeds that we see growing up among the wheat. Jesus said not to do this. We inevitably pull up wheat with the weeds. He said he'd take care of it when he came back.[7]

All three of these temptations play to the best of motives, a desire to defend God's glory and purify his church. But if we fall for any one of them, we'll neither defend his glory nor purify his church. Instead we'll take a giant step toward becoming less like Jesus and more like a Pharisee — a well-intentioned accidental Pharisee perhaps, but a Pharisee nonetheless.

---

4. 2 Cor. 7:4, 13–16; 8:7.
5. 2 Cor. 12:20–21.
6. Mark 3:17; Luke 9:51–56.
7. Matt. 13:24–30.

Discussion Questions for Part 5

IDOLIZING THE PAST

1. Do you ever find yourself guilty of idolizing the past?

    a. If so, what are some of the "good old days" you find yourself longing for? And why?

    b. What are some of the ways that looking at the past through "rose-colored glasses" might warp our perspective? Be as specific as possible.

2. Part 5 discussed the three "whipping boys" that people love to disparage when comparing today to an idealized and idolized past—the church, church leaders, and culture. Which of these three are you most prone to criticize? Why?

3. After reading the chapters in this part, can you think of any great spiritual leaders from the past that you might be putting on a pedestal? If so, who and how so?

4. Why do we tend to remember only the good in our heroes?

    a. How might this be dangerous to our spiritual walk? Be as specific as possible.

b. If someone asked you, "How can we learn from the past without idolizing the past?" what would you tell them?

5. Part 5 ends by summarizing the three great dangers that flow out of an inaccurate and unrealistic idolizing of the past:

- Thinking that the sins and failings of today are unique and rare.

- Lashing out in anger and disgust as if the sins of today are worse than the sins of yesterday.

- Attempting to help Jesus by yanking out the weeds we see growing up among the wheat in the church.

Which, if any, of these three are you most susceptible to? Why?

PART 6

THE QUEST FOR UNIFORMITY

How Uniformity Destroys Unity

CHAPTER 16

UNITY AND UNIFORMITY

How Uniformity Kills Unity

If you're a Christian and I'm a Christian, we're one in Christ. We don't have to produce our unity. We already have it. It's a spiritual reality. But somehow our unity keeps slipping away. It's incredibly elusive. So much so that Jesus prayed that we'd actually experience it, and the Scriptures tell us to work diligently to preserve it. It's awful hard to maintain.[1]

The main reason why can be traced back to page 3 in your Bible. Since Adam's fall, we've had a hard time getting along. His sin messed up everything in this world, including our relationships with one another. So much so that the first story about life outside of the Garden of Eden is the account of one brother killing another—and not surprisingly, it's over the proper way to worship God.[2]

It's no wonder that First Baptist always seems to beget a Second Baptist.

But there is another reason why real and lasting unity is so

---

1. John 17:20–23; Eph. 4:3; 1 Cor. 12:12–13.
2. Genesis 4 tells the story of Cain killing his brother, Abel.

elusive. We often confuse biblical unity with its bogus counterfeit: *uniformity*. It's an age-old problem.

BIBLICAL UNITY

Our biblical unity is a lot like the unity we experience in a family. When my kids were young and crammed into the back seat of our car, they didn't always get along very well. At times they wanted to kill each other. At times I thought they might. But it didn't matter. As I reminded them, they were stuck with each other. They had to learn to get along. They were united by birth, not by choice. And nothing was going to change that.

In the same way, if I'm saved and you're saved (even if I think you barely snuck in), we're family. It doesn't matter if we don't like each other, if we vehemently disagree on all the big issues of the day, or if we've set up warring camps to fight over ancient controversies. We're stuck with each other. We have to learn to get along. We're united by Jesus, not by choice. And nothing is going to change that.

Our biblical unity is rooted solely in our relationship with Jesus. It's not dependent on shared religious practices, patterns, or preferences. It's not contingent on agreeing on every point of theology. It exists even when we wish it didn't.

UNIFORMITY

Uniformity is very different from unity. It's based on clone-like similarities. That's what makes uniformity so comfortable. It's naturally cohesive. When everyone walks, talks, and looks alike, it's not too hard to get along. There aren't so many issues to work through. It's rather easy to be patient, kind, and forbearing with a clone of myself. I understand where you're coming from. I know what you mean. I feel your pain.

But uniformity is not what Jesus died for. He didn't come to break down the dividing walls that separated Jews and Gentiles, slave and free, women and men so that we could coalesce around a boring, blended, homogenous middle. Quite the contrary. He came to save us *in* our differences, not *from* them. God delights in our diversity. Many of our greatest differences are an essential part of his sovereign plan. He actually made us that way—on purpose.[3]

WHEN THE SIBLINGS REFUSE TO GET ALONG

As any parent knows, you can't force your kids to get along. If they want to fight, they'll fight. Dire threats, stiff punishments, and lengthy time-outs may damper the hostilities for a while, but not for long. If you leave the house for a couple of hours and the kids are prone to fight, odds are that when you return, you won't like what happened while you were gone.

Unfortunately, when family members refuse to get along, it's not just the squabbling siblings who suffer. The whole family suffers. It brings shame to the family name. It dishonors the parents. Think back to the last time you saw somebody else's kids having a meltdown in the grocery aisle. My bet is that you didn't think too highly of the children—or the parents. Even if your own kids have had their share of meltdowns in aisle 6, you probably walked away thankful that you weren't part of *that* family.

The same thing happens in the spiritual realm. When the world sees us loving and bearing with one another, like the sons and daughters of God that we are, they're drawn toward us. We gain credibility to speak into their lives. It reflects well on our heavenly Father. But when they see fisticuffs and shouting matches breaking out in the eternal security aisle—or the political aisle, or the Holy Spirit aisle—they can't help but wonder, "What kind of heavenly Father would have a family like that?"

It's no wonder they're not too interested in what we have to say about life, Jesus, or the salvation that we claim we have and that they so desperately need.

WHY WE LOVE BOUNDARY MARKERS

When the quest for uniformity replaces the maintenance of biblical unity, the first thing we tend to do is to establish boundary

---

3. Eph. 2:11–22; 1 Cor. 12:7–31.

markers. Boundary markers are the telling behaviors, symbols, and viewpoints that identify us with one group or another. Show up at a PETA meeting in a fur coat, and it's obvious that you don't belong. Raise your hands too high and jump around too much during worship at First Presbyterian, and it will be clear to all that you're new to the neighborhood—and that you probably moved over from First Pentecostal.

Our actions, dress code, lifestyle, even the vocabulary we use and the things we emphasize, all serve as boundary markers. If your language is earthy, it tells me something. If it's full of God talk and spiritual clichés, it tells me something else. If your church emphasizes reaching seekers or maintaining the conversation or being missional or the need to be more gospel-centered, your choice of code words lets me know instantly which tribe you're from and the theological perspective you bring to the table.

In one sense, boundary markers are unavoidable. In fact, Jesus laid down some rather unequivocal boundary markers when he claimed to be God and said that salvation is found only in him. If you tell me that you think that Jesus was merely a great teacher and that salvation can be found in any sincerely followed religious path, I know which side of the boundary you're on. It's a rather clear indication of where you stand in regard to Christian orthodoxy. I don't need to probe much deeper.

The problem comes when our boundary markers of who's in the kingdom and who's out become narrower than God's. The Pharisees of Jesus' day were masters at establishing these kinds of excessively tight boundary markers. They had a rule and standard for everything, and nearly all of them were designed to quickly establish who was in their tribe and who wasn't.

We become accidental Pharisees when we lay down boundary markers that are narrower than the ones laid down by Jesus and then treat people who line up on the wrong side of *our* markers as if they were spiritual imposters or enemies of the Lord. Our goal may be to protect the flock. But boundary markers that are narrower than the ones Jesus laid down don't *protect* the flock; they *divide* the flock. They sow discord among brothers, something God says he's not too fond of.[4]

They also result in a rash of friendly fire.

THE DAY I FORGOT THE CODE WORDS

I know the pain of friendly fire firsthand. I've been shot at plenty of times. I don't think I'll ever get used to it. It's always a bit disconcerting when people you assume are friends treat you like an enemy.

I remember a number of years ago when I spoke at a pastors' conference for a group I consider myself naturally aligned with. On almost any issue you can name, we see things eye to eye. But I'm not an official member of the tribe. I don't wear the badge. But I could.

My assigned topic was the nuts and bolts of church leadership. My talks were far more Proverbs than Romans, heavier on practical advice than on theology. I thought the sessions went well. That is, until we opened it up for questions and answers. Suddenly I felt like I was in the midst of an inquisition. A small group, perhaps six to ten out of a couple hundred attendees, began to pepper me with questions that were more accusations than questions. It didn't take me long to realize that they hadn't heard a word I'd said. And they weren't about to listen to any of my answers either.

Apparently, without realizing it, I had failed to use some important code words and terminology. No synonyms were allowed. They wanted to hear the *exact* words and phrases. Not only that, I had failed to tack a Bible verse onto *each* of my points. Even worse, I had used some management terms instead of Greek words to describe the dynamics of church leadership.

That put me on the wrong side of my inquisitors' boundary markers. I had failed their vetting process. So they wrote me off as an unbiblical pragmatist, dangerously tempting the other pastors

---

4. Proverbs 6:16–19 lists the things God hates. Included in the list is sowing discord among brothers.

in attendance to replace their full devotion to Jesus and the gospel with a carnal man-centered approach to church ministry.

It was bizarre. I shared their core values (even if I neglected to use the proper buzzwords), and I'm a Bible guy at the core. I usually have a verse for everything, even if I have to use one out of context. It's my background, my personal bent, and it's the way I think. True to form, I actually did have a Bible verse for each of my points. But since I was talking to a roomful of pastors, I assumed I didn't need to quote each one. My bad. Big mistake. Because in the absence of an explicit statement to the contrary, they assumed that anyone who wasn't a card-carrying member of their tribe didn't use the Bible for anything except holding down a nightstand.

That tagged me as a potentially dangerous spiritual imposter. So they fired away. Which is what happens when the comfort zone of uniformity becomes more important than Jesus' command to maintain our unity.

When it comes to our unity in Christ, we constantly have choices to make. How will we respond to our brothers and sisters in Christ we wouldn't have chosen if we had been given the choice—in light of our spiritual unity or in light of our earthly differences? The choice is ours. We can always find a way to get along. We can always find a way to pick a fight. But the choice we make will always have huge ramifications, not only for us but also for all the people we hope to influence and reach for Jesus. They're not too likely to listen when we're beating each other up in aisle 6.

CHAPTER 17

ARE YOUR STUDY NOTES IN RED?

Why the Quest for Theological Uniformity Undercuts the Bible

I had a strange experience a number of years ago. I was a young pastor speaking at a large family camp in Southern California. During one of my talks, I made a couple of mildly controversial statements. Immediately afterward a middle-aged couple came up and asked to speak with me. They were disturbed by what they'd heard. So we walked over to the snack shop to review what I'd said.

We sat down, ordered a shake, and looked up each passage. I pointed out again and again that this was indeed what the Scriptures said. We actually read the verses. But they were not convinced. In fact, the more we talked and the more verses I showed them, the more concerned they became. They were sure I was a false teacher. They warned me not to be unduly influenced by "liberals." They were genuinely concerned for my soul.

Then the oddest thing happened. The wife reached into her carry bag and pulled out a big study Bible. I noticed that it had their favorite pastor's name prominently displayed on the cover.

As my wife and I looked on, they looked up each passage to see what he said in his study notes.

To their shock, he agreed with me on every point.

To my shock, that was the end of the debate.

Suddenly I was a great Bible teacher. Verse after verse of Scripture had left no impact on them. But a couple of confirming sentences from their favorite Bible scholar, and they were thoroughly convinced of the matter.

It was a sad commentary on what inevitably happens when theological uniformity becomes the measure of fidelity to Christ. The Bible is no longer allowed to speak for itself. It needs an approved teacher or textbook to be properly understood.

By the way, before the couple left, I asked if I could see their study Bible for a moment. I wanted to check what color font it used for Jesus' words, because the author's study notes were obviously printed in red.

STUDY NOTES IN RED

Ironically, the more fervently we pursue theological uniformity, the more the Bible takes a back seat, even among people who pride themselves on having the Bible in the navigator's seat. That's because the lens of uniformity insists that everyone interpret difficult or controversial Scripture passages exactly the same way. There's no room for differing opinions, blind spots, or simply being wrong. Those who don't toe the company line are cast aside.

The result is that every time a tough biblical question comes up, we have to consult the tribal manual for the "correct" answer. Instead of our answers and theology flowing out of the Bible, we end up with answers and theological systems superimposed upon the Bible and read back into it. Eventually the Bible becomes nothing more than a proof text for what our tribe already believes.

NOT OF *US* DOESN'T MEAN NOT OF *HIM*

Early in my ministry, I thought that theological uniformity was necessary for ministry cooperation. I believed that it was my duty to carefully watch out for anything in the body of Christ that was slightly out of line, to expose it as widely as possible, and then to drive it out or shut it down as quickly as possible. The underlying assumption was that people who weren't part of our camp or closely aligned with us were against us — and against Jesus as well.

I was shocked to discover that Jesus didn't agree.

He put such thinking to shame when he rebuked some of his disciples for trying to silence a deliverance ministry. They'd come across someone who wasn't part of Jesus' regular entourage casting out demons in his name. They had no idea who he was. They'd never seen him before. Perhaps he was one of those people who sat on the fringe when Jesus taught, soaking it all in but unnoticed by anyone. He must have come to the point of believing in Jesus as the promised Messiah and was now ministering in his name. But since he wasn't part of their official team, the disciples figured there was no way he had the proper credentials or the right to do what he was doing. So John proudly told Jesus, "Master, we saw someone driving out demons in your name and we tried to stop him, because he is not one of us."

But Jesus said, "Do not stop him, for whoever is *not against* you is *for* you." In other words, my kingdom is much bigger than you realize. Don't get in the way of what I'm doing just because I'm not doing it through you.[1]

Jesus' words to the disciples blew up my narrow definition of what constituted an approved ministry. But so did the apostle Paul's response to a group of people who were preaching Christ out of envy, strife, and selfish ambition, trying to stir up trouble for him as he sat in prison. Clearly, they were not in his camp. Clearly, their motivations were out of line. Yet instead of lashing out, Paul took a step back and looked at the bigger picture. "What does it matter?" he wrote. "The important thing is that in every way, whether from false motives or true, Christ is preached. And because of this I rejoice."[2]

---

1. Luke 9:49–50, emphasis added.
2. Phil. 1:15–18.

Wow! Talk about a kingdom attitude!

Jesus and Paul understood a couple of important things that many of us seem to forget in our quest for rigid theological uniformity: (1) God uses people who don't have it all together, and (2) "Not of *us*" doesn't necessarily mean "Not of *him*."

SOME THINGS ARE WORTH FIGHTING OVER

This is not to say that there are never things worth fighting over. Of course there are. Jesus and the Pharisees got into some pretty heated arguments. He said incredibly harsh things about them and their teaching (assuming you consider telling someone they're going to hell to be harsh).[3]

The same was true of the apostle Paul. His rips on the Judaizers are classic. He held nothing back. In response to their insistence that Gentiles had to be circumcised and follow all of the Jewish Old Testament laws in order to be saved, he said he wished they would mutilate themselves. He also said that anyone who presented a false path of salvation should be damned. Then, just for emphasis, he said it again.[4]

Yet there is something important to notice here. In each of these cases (and all of the other New Testament examples of heatedly contending for the gospel), the debate is about the core of salvation. It's not about the nuances. These weren't fierce battles over the fine print, the minute details, or the specifics of the process. They were disputes over who has the right to be saved and what they must do to be saved.

It was the same thing when Jesus went after the Pharisees and religious leaders. They were attempting to keep at bay the sinners he had come to save. This was no minor theological quarrel. It was a matter of eternity and salvation. And that's always worth fighting over. So he embarrassed, ridiculed, and blistered them publically.

---

3. Matthew 23 contains an extended rip on the Pharisees and their teaching.
4. Gal. 1:6–9; 5:12.

But let's be honest. Most of our most heated disputes are not about matters that, when we get them wrong, will send us to hell. Granted, many are about important things—very important things—but it's a stretch to call them eternal. And that's why it's also a stretch to think that God approves when we let our pursuit of theological uniformity escalate to the point that it tears apart his family or closes up the Bible.

CHAPTER 18

AGREEING TO DISAGREE

Why Bearing with One Another Matters

I was once a youth pastor at a church that decided to consider whether to add women to a previously all-male governing board. World War III broke out overnight. Both sides were convinced that God was on their side—and the Devil was on the other side. Lots of Scriptures were tossed around, and nuanced definitions of Greek and Hebrew words were debated late into the night.

The complementarians pointed to all the verses that speak of headship and submission. They argued that the Bible paints a picture of distinctly different but complementary roles for men and women in both the home and the church. They felt it was essential that we keep an all-male board. They were sure that God would remove his presence if we added women.

The egalitarians countered with verses that spoke of our equality in Christ. They argued that there's no distinction between men and women in the Bible. They felt it was essential that we add the women. They were sure that God would start a revival once we got some females on the board.

At one point, a group of church members came and asked me if I would help lead the fight for *our side*. They knew that I had researched the subject and had a strong opinion on it. They wanted me to use my platform as one of the pastors to make sure that *our side* won.

When I said no, they were shocked. Since I had carefully researched the subject, had a strong opinion, and thought it was an important issue, they couldn't understand why I wouldn't pick up the sword to defend what I understood to be the proper application of God's Word.

I told them that it was an easy decision. Even though I had carefully researched the subject and had come to a settled conclusion, people on the other side also loved Scripture, researched it carefully, and sought the leading of the Holy Spirit. They weren't idiots or moral reprobates. The texts weren't indisputable. That's why they're still hotly debated to this day.

More important, there was a long list of crystal-clear commands in my Bible telling me to live in harmony, to be diligent to maintain the unity of the Spirit, to be humble, long-suffering, loving, and forgiving, to bear with my brothers and sisters, and to submit to people in spiritual authority over me. It made no sense to me to disobey this long list of clear commands in order to wage a fierce battle over a handful of verses that were admittedly hard to decipher.

So I told them that I would gladly participate in the debate, but I would not lead the fight. I would say my piece, but then I would seek the peace. If God ever put me in a position where it was my call, I'd make the call. But until then I would try to influence the situation, but I wouldn't help them inflame the situation.

They weren't too happy with my answer. But I think God was.

Today I pastor a church where the makeup of our leadership team reflects my understanding of this hotly debated issue. Yet, interestingly, it's been a nonissue for decades, even though we have lots of folks on both sides of the debate. We've learned to bear with one another, to put first things first, not only on this issue but also on lots of other issues that surface in a place as widely diverse as Southern California.

I've often wondered how much of our remarkable unity can be traced to God's favor with the response I had in my youth pastor days, when I decided to fight for the unity of the body rather than fight for my own preferences and understanding.

Someday I want to ask him. I think he'll say, "Most of it."

THE ZEALOT AND THE TAX COLLECTOR

When we set aside our differences and disagreements to lock arms and march under the banner of Jesus, it authenticates our message of grace, mercy, and forgiveness. It tells a watching world that Jesus really is above all earthly things. That he is Lord of *all*.

I'm convinced that's one of the main reasons why Jesus chose both Simon the Zealot and Matthew the tax collector to be a part of his inner circle. You couldn't find an odder pair. They had nothing in common except an ancestral link to Abraham and a commitment to follow Jesus. Other than that, they were natural enemies.

Simon was a Zealot, a member of a Jewish revolutionary group dedicated to overthrowing their Roman oppressors. Most Jews saw him as a heroic freedom fighter. Most Romans saw him as a crazy nationalistic insurrectionist.

Matthew, on the other hand, was a tax collector for the Roman government. He gathered exorbitant taxes from his fellow Jews and then handed the money over to their Roman oppressors. Most Jews saw him as a despicable traitor. Most Romans saw him as a sensible and compliant member of a conquered nation.

In the natural order of things, Simon and Matthew would have hated each other. Yet when Jesus called them to follow him (and later to become two of his twelve apostles), they set aside their differences and leaped at the opportunity. Imagine what a strong impression that must have made on the crowds that came to see and hear Jesus. Not only was he a miracle worker, not only did he speak with astonishing authority; his entourage included a Zealot and a tax collector!

For most Jews, that had to rank right up there with Jesus' other miracles, perhaps a step or two behind raising the dead, but definitely more amazing than restoring sight to the blind.

A SHOCKINGLY DIVERSE CONGREGATION

This same kind of astonishing unity was also modeled by the early church. It's hard to overstate how shocking it must have been to see Jews and Gentiles, slave and free, men and women crowded into a house to worship Jesus. In a culture built around class distinctions, citizenship status, and uncrossable social boundaries, this had to be mind-boggling. Jesus' ability to unite a group of people so eclectic (and normally hostile toward one another) spoke volumes about his authority and supremacy. It gave credence to the claims that he was indeed the risen Son of God.

Today we place lots of emphasis on increasing racial diversity in our churches. That's a good thing. It's needed. But there's more to having a genuinely mosaic church than just racial and socioeconomic diversity. We also have to learn to work through the passionate and mutually exclusive opinions that we have in the realms of politics, theology, and ministry priorities.

The world is watching to see if our modern-day Simon the Zealots and Matthew the tax collectors can learn to get along for the sake of the Lord Jesus. If not, we shouldn't be surprised if it no longer listens to us. Jesus warned us that people would have a hard time believing that he was the Son of God and that we were his followers if we couldn't get along. Whenever we fail to play nice in the sandbox, we give people on the outside good reason to write us off, shake their heads in disgust, and ask, "What kind of Father would have a family like that?"[1]

BEARING WITH ONE ANOTHER

To create and maintain the kind of unity that exalts Jesus as Lord of *all*, we have to learn what it means to genuinely bear with one

---

1. John 13:34–35; 17:22–23. According to Jesus, if we love one another, the world will know that we are his disciples. If we live in unity, the world will know that the Father sent him and loved him.

another. I fear that for lots of Christians today, bearing with one another is nothing more than a cliché, a verse to be memorized but not a command to obey.[2]

By definition, bearing with one another is an act of selfless obedience. It means dying to self and overlooking things I'd rather not overlook. It means working out real and deep differences and disagreements. It means offering to others the same grace, mercy, and patience when they are dead wrong as Jesus offers to me when I'm dead wrong.

As I've said before, I'm not talking about overlooking heresy, embracing a different gospel, or ignoring high-handed sin. But I am talking about agreeing to disagree on matters of substance and things we feel passionate about. If we overlook only the little stuff, we aren't bearing with one another. We're just showing common courtesy.

THE WORST DOGFIGHTS

It's strange, but it's often hardest to bear with people who are closest to us. Many of us do a better job of bearing with non-Christians than we do of bearing with our annoying and wrongheaded brothers and sisters in Christ. Our meanest and nastiest fights are often with members of the same tribe we belong to. We've been known to eat our own.

In that sense, we can be a lot like the Pharisees of Jesus' day. They didn't just look down on the masses; they also disdained some of their fellow Pharisees. It wasn't enough to be a Pharisee. You had to be the *right kind* of Pharisee.

I find that not much has changed today. People who think of themselves as well-taught and deeply committed Christians often aren't satisfied to ask me if I'm a fellow Christian. They want to know if I'm the *right kind* of Christian. They have nine follow-up questions just to be sure. And I'd better get all of my answers right.

That's a tragedy, because it destroys our unity in Christ and replaces it with its bogus substitute: uniformity. It takes God's glorious kingdom and breaks it down into little fiefdoms constantly warring with one another.

---

2. Col. 3:13; Eph. 4:1–3.

SOME CLICHÉS ARE TRUE

So how do we actually bear with one another in a way that doesn't sweep our significant and very real differences under the carpet or treat critical issues as unimportant?

I've found that there is an old cliché that helps. You've probably heard it before. "Hate the sin, but love the sinner." It's usually applied to our relationship with people outside the faith. But it also needs to be applied to our fellow believers who have some inane viewpoints, sloppy theology, and embarrassing practices.

The apostle John put it this way: "Anyone who claims to be in the light but hates a brother or sister is still in the darkness. Anyone who loves their brother and sister lives in the light, and there is nothing in them to make them stumble. But anyone who hates a brother or sister is in the darkness and walks around in the darkness. They do not know where they are going, because the darkness has blinded them."[3]

I used to read this passage and feel pretty good about myself. I thought, "I don't hate anyone. That's an awful strong word." But then I discovered that the Greek word John uses in this passage *(miseo)* doesn't refer to murderous hatred. It simply means to detest someone or something.

I no longer felt so good about myself. In fact, I remember the first time I realized the full implication of this passage and the meaning of that word. All I could say was, "Forgive me, Lord!"

Ultimately, we all have a choice to make.

We can live in light of our spiritual unity, or we can live in denial of it. We can focus on our common allegiance to Jesus, or we can focus on our many areas of significant disagreement. We can bear with one another, or we can fight and divide. We can sow the seeds of brotherly love, or we can sow the seeds of discord. We can cause people to say, "My, how they love one another," or we can cause them to say, "What kind of God has a family like that?"

---

3. 1 John 2:9–11.

Discussion Questions for Part 6

THE QUEST FOR UNIFORMITY

1. After reading part 6, how, in your own words, would you define the difference between *uniformity* and *unity?*

2. Have you ever seen firsthand a situation where the quest for uniformity destroyed the potential for biblical unity? If so, what happened? What did you learn?

3. If you had to name your tribe's boundary markers, code words, and "red-word" teachers, what would that list look like? Be as specific as possible.

   a. How would someone from outside your tribe learn about those things if he or she wanted to fit in?

   b. Would the Jesus of the New Testament be inside or outside of those boundaries?

4. As we saw, there are some things that are worth fighting for. Which specific issues do you believe should be on that list? What filter do you use to decide when an issue is worth fighting for and when it's best to "agree to disagree"?

5. On a scale from 0 (we are clones) to 10 (we are shockingly different), how would you rate the diversity (not just racial diversity) of your congregation? How would you rate the Christian diversity of your personal relationships, circles of friends, and colleagues?

6. Looking back over the chapters in part 6, what one thing most jumps out at you as a new insight or an important principle? Why? How do you plan to respond to it?

PART 7

GIFT PROJECTION

When My Calling Becomes
Everyone Else's Calling

CHAPTER 19

CHOCOLATE-COVERED ARROGANCE

The Dark Side of Gift Projection

From my earliest days as a Christ follower, I had an insatiable appetite for Scripture. I'd stay up late into the night reading, looking up cross-references, and jotting down notes in the margin. I could close my eyes and remember where a particular verse was on a page.

I thought everyone could.

I saw my hunger for God's Word as a sign of my superior dedication to Jesus. I couldn't understand how someone could be saved and not have a deep craving to comprehend all that the Bible has to say. I considered people who failed to study it in depth spiritually tepid and lazy.

It never dawned on me that my growing hunger for God's Word might be connected to my spiritual gifts and God's future calling on my life. As I look back, it only makes sense that God would give me a passion for the book he wanted me to teach. But in my immaturity, I didn't see my hunger as a God-given desire for a God-given assignment. I saw it as a sign of my superior spiritual zeal.

I didn't know it at the time, but I had a bad case of gift projection, the chocolate-covered arrogance that assumes that everyone is just like me — or will be when they grow up — and whatever God has gifted and called me to do, everyone else should do as well.

LOW-LEVEL GIFT PROJECTION

Most of us have some degree of low-level gift projection. It's hard not to. We all see and interpret life through the lens of our own experiences. It's the only lens we have. So it's natural to expect that others see and feel the same things we do.

For example, consider the way that most of us raise our children or try to disciple a new believer. We focus primarily on making sure that they are exposed to the right information and the right experiences. We treat them as blank slates waiting to be programmed. We assume that information and environment trumps genes and personality.

But that's not how life works. We aren't blank slates. Each of us has our own unique set of genetics, personality traits, and spiritual gifting, not to mention a sin nature that puts static on the line. That's why no two of us ever respond to the same set of stimuli in the same way. The fact is, if you lived exactly the life I've lived (knowing what I know and experiencing everything I've experienced), you still wouldn't be me — or agree with me on everything. We're different.

But that's a hard lesson to learn. It's counter to how most of us view life. I remember when my oldest son, Nathan, was born. My wife and I thought it would be a good idea if he grew up eating healthy and shunning violence. So we kept him away from sugars, toy guns, and most television. We figured a well-controlled environment would easily trump genetics and human nature. To that end, we have a pathetic picture of him on his first birthday. He's surrounded by politically correct toys and a sugar-free carrot muffin with a candle stuck in it.

A lot of good that did.

It wasn't long before every stick turned into a lightsaber or a stun gun. When his grandma asked him what he wanted for Christmas, he told her, "Weapons!"

By the time our third child reached his first birthday, we had learned our lesson. Our kids weren't wet cement. We could influence, but we couldn't control. So we went ahead and served him chocolate cake with lard-based frosting. I think we also bought him a toy tank and a Glock.

While this kind of low-level gift projection can lead to some unrealistic expectations, cookie-cutter discipleship, and frustration with people who don't respond as we think they should, it won't derail our walk with God. It won't tear apart the body of Christ.

Not so with full-blown gift projection. It's nasty. I call it chocolate-covered arrogance because from the outside it looks like healthy spiritual zeal, but on the inside it's nothing but sinful pride and arrogance. It causes us to look down on others, sows discord, and produces lots of false guilt. Even worse, the more full-blown our gift projection becomes, the more likely we are to think that God is especially pleased with us and ticked off at everyone else, when nothing could be farther from the truth.

FULL-BLOWN GIFT PROJECTION

The first thing to understand about full-blown gift projection is that it's a sin of the spiritually passionate. You won't find it among the apathetic or lukewarm. It's found only among the zealous and highly committed, people who most want to please the Lord.

The problem isn't spiritual zeal. We're called to be zealous.[1] The problem comes when we mix our spiritual zeal with the hyperindividualized spirituality that characterizes much of American Christianity. It's a toxic combination.

Let me explain.

It's All about Me

Most of us tend to read every *you* in the Bible as if it were a first-person singular pronoun, even though most are plurals (the

---

1. Rom. 12:11.

Southern *y'all*). We treat every promise and command as if it were ours, aimed directly at us and our circumstances. We pay little attention to the historical context or to the actual people to whom a specific command or promise was originally directed.

On one level, that can be a good thing, if it causes us to treat our Bibles as a life manual. But on another level, it can be a bad thing, especially when it fosters a skewed, "I'm at the center of God's universe" spirituality.

For instance, if we're caught in the middle of a downpour and need a parking spot by the front door, an "I'm at the center of God's universe" spirituality sees God as directly causing someone to leave the store, get in their car, and pull out just as we drive by. We chalk it up as a sign of his loving-kindness. And if a space doesn't open up, we assume that God kept everyone in the store a little longer so we could grow in our patience and character.

Now, I'm not arguing that God doesn't know or care about us as individuals. Of course he does. Maybe he gives us parking spaces. I don't know. But I guarantee you that the persecuted saints in other parts of the world would be amazed at our concept of a parking attendant God whose primary way of producing patience and character in our life is to make us walk a few hundred feet in the rain.

Here's why this warning about hyperindividualized spirituality is so important. If we allow it to take root in our life and then combine it with a zealous pursuit of God's calling on our life, it's almost impossible to avoid falling into the trap of full-blown gift projection. After all, if I think I'm at the epicenter of the universe, it's only logical that my gifts and calling are as well.

I Don't Need You

Once we begin to think that way, it's only a matter of time before we begin to castigate and write off people with gifts and callings that don't match ours. To borrow the apostle Paul's analogy of the body of Christ, the process usually goes something like this:

If you're an eye, you'll start to devalue the ears as ancillary and second-class appendages because they can't see anything. You'll attend some special vision conferences where you'll gather with other eyes to celebrate the beauty of sight, learn new ways to sharpen your vision, and listen to guest eyes bemoan the terrible blindness that ails the rest of the body. Eventually you'll join a vision-focused church where you can study the latest in biblical optometry and congratulate yourself for your clarity of vision in a world gone blind—all the while hardly noticing that you and your eye friends can no longer do much besides see. You have no feet for walking, no mouth for talking, and no ears to hear anything but your own thoughts.[2]

If you ever see this pattern starting to form in your life, I warn you. Run! You'll recognize it by a growing frustration with people who aren't just like you. Get as far away as possible from those who share your gift and calling until you've regained your appreciation for the beauty and majesty of the entire body of Christ. Then head back to what God has called and gifted you to do, with a spirit of humility rather than the prideful zeal of gift projection.

THE FLAVOR OF THE DAY

Here's something else I've noticed. Secular culture has a lot more to do with which spiritual gifts and callings get put up on a pedestal than most of us realize. Those that line up best with the values and passions of the day become the flavor of the day.

For instance, in the era of colonialism, people who were called to the foreign mission field were considered to be the quintessential example of spiritual commitment. Their willingness to leave everything behind in order to expand the frontiers of God's kingdom fit in well with the prevailing values of the day. It's no wonder that sermons, books, and conferences lifted up overseas missions as the one calling that every Christian needed to seriously consider. In fact, it was pretty much taken for granted that God was calling everyone to go; the only question was, Who was dedicated enough to heed the call?

Fast-forward to the 1980s and 1990s. Our culture is now enamored with strong and successful leaders. Everyone wants to

---

2. 1 Cor. 12:7–27.

get an MBA. Books and conferences on leadership sell out. Mission conferences languish. Suddenly the spiritual gift of leadership becomes the flavor of the day.[3] Gifted leaders write books and tell packed-out conferences that anyone can become a great leader if they're willing to work hard, gain some leadership wisdom, and give themselves completely to the Lord. People who toil faithfully in obscurity with little fruit are no longer considered faithful (as they were in the foreign missions era). They're considered ineffective. They're written off as losers.

More recently our culture has shifted again. This time, we've fallen in love with causes. Everyone sports a wristband, has a favorite charity, and if you don't, they wonder why. Even large corporations have jumped on the bandwagon. They all want to be seen as socially responsible. It's no surprise that people who've been called to serve on the front lines of mercy and justice ministries are the new darlings of the day. Their willingness to make financial sacrifices, go overseas, or move into the inner city fits perfectly with the social awareness of our culture. So they've become the latest mold into which everyone must fit in order to be classified as a committed Christ follower.

If your gifts and calling happen to align with the flavor of the day, you can expect lots of encouragement and support. You'll be put on a pedestal. But be forewarned. You'll also be sorely tempted toward some serious gift projection.

If your gifts and calling don't happen to fit with the flavor of the day, you can expect some serious self-doubt, a lot of criticism, and little understanding from people who don't consider your gifts and calling to be very important.

NEEDLESS GUILT

The final thing to understand about the dark side of gift projection is that it's not a victimless sin. It doesn't just hurt those of us who puff up with the pride of gift projection. It hurts the people we project upon. It creates a lot of needless guilt.

---

3. Rom. 12:6–8.

I see this every time a new "you aren't doing enough for God" book hits the bestseller list. My inbox fills with the plaintive pleas of guilt-ridden friends and church members who want to serve God with everything they have but don't have the same gifts, calling, or opportunity as the author they just read or speaker they just heard. These are stellar Christians (the halfhearted never worry about this stuff) beaten down by the gift projection of an articulate author or speaker. So they write me emails like the following:[4]

Dear Pastor,

I just finished reading [fill in the name of any popular "you need to do what I've been called to do" book], and I'm so deeply disturbed that I'm having a hard time concentrating on anything.

We are not rich by American standards, and most people would not consider us materialistic. We make about $32,000 a year. We tithe, live on hand-me-down-clothing, and support one child overseas. We don't use credit cards at all and we are debt free, so we're being responsible. But we're crunched financially.

Still, we do have a house, we've never gone hungry, and we have clean water when others don't. And we still buy things for pleasure like makeup for me, a stuffed animal for Callie, and a video game for Jacob. Is this okay when people are starving? Where is the line?

The scariest thought: Am I the rich young ruler? I don't think I can say that I'll give up *all* of my possessions for the poor and follow Him. Just writing this makes my stomach turn. But I have to be brutally honest with myself. I'm messing with eternity here. I don't want to get that wrong.

I remember reading something about John Wesley living on $28 a month because that's all he needed to survive, and he gave the rest away. I admit that I cringe at the thought ...

---

4. These are excerpted from real letters and emails slightly altered to protect the identity and confidentiality of the sender.

and then I cringe at the fact that I cringed. I'm stuck. What should I do?

Here's another one.

Pastor,

I have something to ask you. I claim that I've given my life as a living sacrifice, yet I still do some extracurricular activities like surfing, fixing up my home, hobbies, and going to the movies after work. Is that okay? Or should I stop wasting my time on these things and spend more time serving God? I don't want to disappoint him. I feel like I need some time for myself. But maybe I don't.

And here are two more.

Pastor,

I take care of my home, husband, and kids. I also volunteer at the church every other week, visit my mom who has Alzheimer's, and help my friends. Is it okay if I take my spare time and do something for myself once in a while? Sometimes I'm so tired serving God that I don't know what to do. I know I shouldn't be, but I am. I'm worried that when I get to heaven, I'll find out that I was storing up trinkets.

Pastor,

I just read [fill in the blank], and now I'm really concerned. I don't know what to do. I'm stuck in a dead-end job, actually two of them, as I have to work a second job to pay our rent and my wife's school debt. I feel like we should give more, but we hardly make it as is. I also think I need to go on that missions trip to Haiti next month, but my boss won't let me have any time off until I've been here a year, and I know my wife is going to want me to spend my vacation time with her and the kids. Is Jesus okay with that? I know I should do more. But I don't know how.

Emails like that break my heart. I believe they break Jesus' heart too. He told the weary and heavily burdened to come to him for rest. He promised a lighter load and an easier yoke. It was the Pharisees of his day who constantly increased the burdens on the people and endlessly called for more. The accidental Pharisees of our day continue to do the same.

The Bible calls Satan the accuser of the brethren.[5] Jesus is called our advocate.[6] If you find yourself prone to gift-projection, remember whose work you are doing. There is no more dangerous place to be than sitting in the seat of an accidental Pharisee, pretending to know and dispense God's will for everyone else.

And if you find yourself prone to take on the gift projections of others, remember that God wants you to do what he has gifted and called you to do, not what everyone else wants you to do. There is no better place to be than at the center of his will, using your gifts and fulfilling your calling to his glory.

It may not always be easy to be a foot in a world of hands. But if God has made you to be a foot in the body of Christ, don't try to be a hand. Granted, the hands might not think all that highly of you and what you do. But trust me, they'll never go very far without you.

5. Rev. 12:10.
6. 1 John 2:1.

CHAPTER 20

GIFT ENVY AND DRIVE-BY GUILTINGS

Why Evangelists, Missionaries, and Bible Teachers Make Us Feel Guilty

My evangelistically gifted friends make me feel guilty. Sometimes it's on purpose. But most of the time it's unintentional. It's just the way they are, and the way I'm not.

When they walk into a restaurant, they immediately steer the conversation toward spiritual things. They're disappointed if their waitress doesn't receive Christ before the meal is over. They'll order dessert just to have one more chance to share the gospel.

Meanwhile, when I walk into a restaurant, I'm looking for a good seat. If I try to engage the waitress in a significant spiritual conversation, she thinks I'm hitting on her. She's more likely to bring over the manager than pray to receive Christ. When I order dessert, it's because I'm a sucker for ice cream.

The same goes for airplanes. My evangelistically gifted friends pray for a hard-core pagan to sit next to them. Then they lead him to Christ. I pray for the seat next to me to stay empty. Then a fat guy with BO sits there with his headphones on the whole time.

I also hide in the closet whenever two guys in white shirts on bicycles turn into my driveway. I stay until they leave.

To my evangelistically gifted friends, these are sure signs that I don't care about the lost and that I fail to understand the gravity of eternity. Otherwise I'd lead waitresses to Christ, pray for lost people to sit next to me on airplanes, and flag down the guys on bicycles.

So they pray for me. A lot.

But most of the guilt I feel for not being more aggressively evangelistic is not my friends' fault. They certainly have some low-level gift projections they put on me (don't we all), but it's not the full-blown, sinfully arrogant type. No, that's not why I feel guilty. I feel guilty because I often struggle with *gift envy*. I bet many of you do as well.

GIFT ENVY

Gift envy is the flip side of gift projection. It's usually applied to something we think is especially important in the kingdom of God and wish we were better at.

For me, evangelism fits the bill. Now, don't get me wrong. I share my faith. I've led plenty of people to Christ. It's hard to be a pastor and not have a concern for the lost and a gift to reach them. But when it comes to talking to complete strangers about Jesus or being evangelistically assertive, I'm tongue-tied. My gift for gab goes out the window. Perhaps you're shy around strangers, don't think well on your feet, desire to actually know the questions before giving answers, or have a hard time remembering all the cool apologetics you learned when your small group studied *How to Share Your Faith Like a Real Christian*. If so, you know what I'm talking about.

The same kind of gift envy happens with Bible teachers, missionaries, and spiritual risk-takers. Because most of us value knowing God's Word, reaching the lost, and stepping out in faith, folks with these gifts can stir up some significant gift envy in the rest of us.

So let's look at each of these to figure out why so many of us feel like spiritual trash and wish we were someone else when we hang around people with these high-profile gifts and callings. It starts with an understanding of the unique power and dangers that come with their public platform.

Public Platforms

Evangelists, pastors, teachers, ministry leaders, church planters, and missionaries have a public platform that makes it easy for them to present a model of discipleship that looks an awful lot like them. Their self-congratulatory stories and natural built-in bias toward what God has called them to do can leave the rest of us wondering what's wrong with us.

By the way, I'm not suggesting that people with background gifts wouldn't do the same thing if they had a platform. We're all tempted to define spirituality and discipleship in ways that align perfectly with who we are and what we do. But those with up-front gifts are the ones who have the platform. So they're the ones who set the agenda.

Evangelists

Evangelists have a hard time remembering that most people aren't wired like them. They forget that their comfort in talking to strangers is a God-given gift. Most of us will never be comfortable talking to total strangers or aggressively turning the conversation toward spiritual things. Few of us will ever master the sales pitch and know how to close the deal.

That's not sin. That's not spiritual apathy. It's the way God made us. He made half of us to be introverts. On purpose. It wasn't a mistake.

We need evangelists to do what they do. Whether they're boldly and successfully sharing their faith in the marketplace, overseas, as a church planter, or in some other way, they're incredibly important to the kingdom. They're on the front lines of the Great Commission. Without them it limps along.

But it's also important to remember that God hasn't called and gifted all of us to be evangelists (despite what our evangelistically gifted friends may think). Instead he's called all of us to show our workplace, community, and neighborhood the love of Christ and to live such good lives that they stand up and take notice, to tell our story when asked, and to be willing to say, "Come and see" even when we don't have much to say after that.[1] But we don't have to go about it like an evangelist. We don't have to have all the answers. And we should never feel guilty about being who God made us to be or doing what he called us to do. If he wanted you to be an evangelist, he would have made you one.

Bible Teachers

Bible teachers also have a built-in platform from which to fire guilt-seeking missiles. If you teach the Bible at any level, you'll be tempted to look down on people who don't know what you know. You'll have a hard time imagining that God could be pleased with anyone who isn't conversant with the finer points of theology. And you'll probably think that everyone needs to know the general outline and theme of every book in the Bible. All sixty-six. Including Zephaniah.

Not long ago I read a quote from a nationally known Bible scholar who claimed that a deep and accurate theology was essential in order to be an effective parent. He seems to believe that it's hard to be a good dad without a robust theology.

I found his statement odd, because despite his own robust theology, he's not been much of a husband or father. To his credit, he's admitted it in numerous public settings. But to his discredit, he still projects his gifts and calling on everyone else.

Now, I'm not opposed to rigorous theological training. I have three earned degrees. I teach seminary classes. I know that a messed-up theology can lead to a messed-up life. But I also know that despite what many of my fellow pastors, seminary profs, and colleagues may think, it's possible to live a vibrant Christian life and be a godly parent even if you know a lot more about the theology of Bart Simpson than about the theology of Karl Barth.

And if you happen to be one of the many Christ followers who feel like a spiritual loser because you don't know all the big

---

1. 1 Peter 2:11–15; 3:15.

words, mispronounce the names of Hebrew kings, and have to use your table of contents to look up cross-references, take hope. Jesus once thanked his heavenly Father for hiding the meaning of his teaching from the wise and learned and instead revealing it to little children. I don't think any of those children had a robust theology. And they were also the ones whom Jesus said the kingdom of heaven belongs to.[2]

Missionaries and Risk Takers

But no one gets put on a pedestal like missionaries and risk takers. In many Christian circles, they're considered to be the ultimate example of spiritual dedication and sacrifice. Their willingness to leave the comfort zone in order to advance the cause of the kingdom gives them an aura of being far more committed than the rest of us.

But they aren't more committed. They're simply fulfilling their gifts and calling. Even more to the point, if you *haven't* been specifically gifted and called to go to the mission field or to take a big risk for the kingdom of God and you do so anyway, you'll be out of God's will.

That's right. You'll be out of God's will.

Unfortunately, that message is seldom heard today. Instead we're bombarded with the gift projections of people who have been called to go and then asked to come back and speak. They implore us to do what they've done, implying that if we don't, we're either not listening to God or selfishly clinging to the comforts of this world instead of seeking the kingdom of God.

It's no wonder so many of us feel terminally guilty.

Faith and Risk

Missionaries and risk takers love to say things like, "If you don't currently have some area of your life where you will fail miserably if God doesn't intervene, you're not living by faith." To a natural-born risk taker, that makes perfect sense. It's where the adventuresome live. They find routine and predictability to be

---

2. Matt. 11:25–26; 19:14.

worse than hell itself. They fear the land of the bland. They'd rather die than be bored. They equate living on the edge with living by faith.

But if that's your bent, be careful spouting such nonsense. Because nowhere in the Bible are we called to be adventuresome and risk-taking. We're called to be obedient. That might entail great adventure and risk. But it also might entail a life of routine and predictability. It's God's call, not ours.

Consider for a moment the great stories of faith in Hebrews 11. There's not one example of someone going out on a limb to see if God would rescue them. These heroes of the faith weren't taking crazy risks; they were merely doing what God explicitly told them to do. Nothing more. Nothing less.

Over the years, I've had lots of people come into my office convinced that God wanted them to do something cuckoo. But it's never been because of a biblical command, a specific vision from God, or the advice of godly counsel. It's always the same story. They think that God will reward them for doing something risky (or stupid). So they take the leap. Sadly, in most cases we don't meet again for quite a while. And when they do come back in, it's usually to ask for help putting their shattered finances, marriage, or life back together.

If you're hardwired for adventure and risk taking, don't play it safe. That's not how God made you. But don't judge the spirituality of others through the lens of God's calling on your life. Despite what you may think, you're not living on the ragged edge because you have greater faith. You live there because God wired you for risk and adventure.

If you're the type who's scared to death by risk, don't sweat it. There's no reason to feel guilty because you don't want to go stop sex trafficking in Bangkok, wade your way through the Amazon jungle, or spend your summer digging wells in Africa. Stick with what you've been called to do. If God wants you to take a risk, he'll give you the will and the power to pull it off.[3] He promised. And he won't need any drive-by guiltings to get his message across.

---

3. Phil. 2:13.

THE MYTH OF "FULL-TIME" MINISTRY

Lots of baseless guilt and gift envy can be traced to the fallout from an unfortunate term that has found its way deep into our Christian vocabulary: *full-time ministry*. It implies that people who make their living in ministry are somehow serving God full-time while the rest of us serve him in our spare time.

That's pure baloney.

If you are a Christian, you're in full-time ministry. You are a believer-priest on special assignment representing God in everything you do.[4] The only difference between those of us who serve God in so-called full-time ministry and those of us who serve him in the secular marketplace is the organization that pays our salary and the setting in which we carry out our ministry.

If you stock shelves at Walmart, run a pool-cleaning service, or crunch numbers in a cubical, you're in full-time ministry. Your assignment is to infiltrate a segment of society that would otherwise go untouched. What you do is every bit as important to the kingdom as anything done by people who get their paycheck from a church or ministry organization.

Unfortunately, that's a message seldom heard. Most Christians have an inadequate and incomplete theology of work. We think some things are spiritual and some things are secular.[5]

What's Wrong with Selling Shoes for Jesus?

For example, a number of years ago a prominent and highly gifted pastor got busted for an affair. Not long afterward he was offered a teaching position at another high-profile church. When the pastor who hired him was asked why he hired him so quickly, he said, "This man is simply too gifted to waste his time selling shoes."

I'm not kidding. He really said that. And he said it to his entire congregation.

Imagine how the shoe salesmen in his church must have felt.

No wonder our churches are full of people who serve God

---

4. Col. 3:17; 1 Peter 2:9–10.

5. For a helpful discussion of this issue, see Tom Nelson's book *Work Matters: Connecting Sunday Worship to Monday Work* (Wheaton, Ill.: Crossway, 2012).

with distinction in the marketplace but feel like spiritual garbage. They've been told too many times that serving God in the marketplace and in their neighborhoods is a second-class job in the kingdom.

The Curse of Adulation and Special Treatment

The concept of full-time ministry creates other problems as well. It often brings with it special perks and privileges that can poison the soul. Like the Pharisees of old, those of us in full-time ministry can fall in love with the special greetings in the marketplace, the best seats at the banquets, and the praise of the people.[6]

The result is often a leader who loves to pontificate on the beauty of servant-leadership but never experiences anything close to it.[7] It also causes many in professional ministry to become accidental Pharisees, addicted to the perks and adulation that come with the role, insisting on fancy titles, special discounts, and the honor they think they're due.

So here's my advice if you're in a full-time ministry role: Enjoy the perks of ministry when they come your way as a grace gift. But run from them the moment they become an expectation. They will rot your soul.

The Trap of Special Exemptions

Another danger for people who serve in full-time ministry is the false assumption that their "extra sacrifices" exempt them from the responsibilities required of everyone else.

For instance, a few weeks ago a pastor friend of mine discovered that the vast majority of his ministry staff have not given a dime to the ministry. They think they are making less money than they would in the business world (a very disputable assumption, as many who've lost their job in a church or ministry have found out to their surprise). So they think they're exempt from the requirement to be financially generous.

---

6. Luke 11:43.
7. Matt. 20:25–28.

Of course, the same could be said by every person who works in a nonprofit, the social sector, the military, or teaches in a school. And what about people with minimum-wage jobs? Are all of these folks exempt from the requirement to be generous and store up heavenly treasures?

Jesus didn't seem to think so. He praised the generosity of a destitute widow who put all she had into the temple treasury. If her poverty had exempted her, he should have thanked her and then refunded her contribution.[8]

Or consider the Levite priests. Even though they weren't allowed to own property and lived off the tithes of the people, the Old Testament laws didn't let them off the generosity hook. They were still required to contribute a tithe out of the tithe they received.[9]

But that's what happens when we elevate the sacrifices of people in so-called full-time ministry. It causes them to think they're something special—a better and more committed brand of Christians, deserving a few special waivers and exemptions.

THE SURPRISING TRUTH ABOUT HONOR AND PRAISE

Perhaps the greatest irony of gift projection and gift envy is that God has specifically arranged the body of Christ so that people who receive greater honor and prestige are actually the least important and necessary.

In his first letter to the Corinthians, the apostle Paul said that the body of Christ is just like our physical bodies. The parts we notice, honor, and praise are the parts that matter the least.[10] For instance, you'll never make the cover of a glamour magazine because you have a marvelous liver, kidney, or pancreas. You might make it if you've got great hair, beautiful eyes, a fabulous complexion, a body that won't quit, or killer abs.

---

8. Luke 21:1–4.
9. Num. 18:26.
10. 1 Cor. 12:22–25.

But none of those are very important to life itself. You can live a long and productive life with a rat's nest of unmanageable hair, a homely face, and a pear-shaped body. But you won't survive long with a diseased heart, a poorly functioning liver, or a failing pancreas.

In the same way, the body of Christ can go a long way without the gifts that get most of the glory and without the roles we tend to envy. Just look at the persecuted church. Every time the platformed gifts are forced underground, the church goes on just fine — some would even say better.

CHAPTER 21

MONEY POLICE

What Ever Happened to the Epistles?

There is one final group of gift projectors who need their own chapter. They're deeply committed to Jesus, mercy, and justice. They're incredibly sacrificial and generous. But they're also myopic. Mr. Magoo myopic. They see the whole world through the lens of their passion and calling. They have little patience (and no respect) for people who don't share the same lens and the same calling.

They are the *money police*.

They have an uncanny ability to know God's plan for every penny they have — and every penny you and I have as well. They're the ultimate gift projectors. If you don't line up with their standard of generosity, they won't just criticize you. They'll question your salvation.

WHERE DO THEY COME FROM?

Most of the money police I've known start out with the best of intentions. They want to advance the kingdom, promote genuine discipleship, help the needy, and fulfill the mission of God.

Many of them come at it by way of their own generosity. They often have what Romans 12:8 calls a gift of giving. They see needs, are stirred by the Spirit to meet those needs, and find great joy and fulfillment in doing so. But as with everyone when it comes to using spiritual gifts, they seldom think they are doing anything out of the ordinary. They think they are doing what all of us should do. And they're not shy to let it be known.[1]

Others come at it by way of a strong bent toward idealism. Often they're students or young singles who've read a book, taken a short-term mission trip, or attended a conference that opened their eyes to the needs of the world. Ironically, I've found that many of them have no history of personal generosity, yet they're quick to judge the financial priorities and motives of others. It's kind of strange. I often wonder what they'll do when they have real money of their own, spouses and children to provide for, and a retirement to prepare for. I hope they'll live out the radical generosity they currently expect of others, because Jesus said that we'll all be judged in light of how we judge others.[2]

Armed with a few favorite verses and Jesus stories, these folks are hard to argue with. If you point out the inconsistencies in their use of Scripture, question the context of a favorite passage, or challenge their conclusions, they'll write you off as a materialistic bogus Christian who rationalizes away the hard sayings of Jesus.

It reminds me of debating with someone who believes in a conspiracy theory. There is no way to win the argument. If you show them that there's no credible evidence for their theory, they'll write you off as naive and claim that the lack of evidence is actually proof of the conspiracy. It shows how well it's been covered up.

CUT-AND-PASTE THEOLOGY

The first problem with the way today's money police use Scripture is their tendency to cut and paste. They love the words of

---

1. Listings of the spiritual gifts can be found in 1 Corinthians 12, Romans 12, Ephesians 4, and 1 Peter 4.
2. Matt. 7:1–2.

Jesus and of the minor prophets. They don't seem to have nearly as much interest in the New Testament letters. Though they don't realize it, their approach to Scripture is a lot like that of the ancient Pharisees and the religious elite. They too were masters of cut-and-paste theology.

The Pharisees and the Law

The Pharisees and religious scholars of Jesus' day thought of themselves as deeply committed to Scripture. But in reality, they spent most of their time dialed in on the first five books of the Old Testament. They pretty much ignored the prophets—except when they were trying to kill them.

For instance, when the wise men showed up in Jerusalem asking where the king of the Jews would be born, the Pharisees and religious scholars knew enough to point to Micah's prophecy that he would be born in Bethlehem.[3] But they had no interest in following up to see what God might be up to. They were too busy arguing over how to apply the letter of the law to all the commands found in the first five books.

Their battles with Jesus over healing on the Sabbath are another illustration of their pick-and-choose theology. They'd thought long and hard about the Sabbath rules, but they never connected them to what the prophets said about God's desiring mercy over sacrifice.[4]

I find that today's money police do much the same thing. They fixate on every word of Jesus. But they seldom check out the New Testament letters to see how the apostles interpreted Jesus' words and applied them to the life of the early church.

What Ever Happened to the Epistles?

All of Scripture is God's Word. No part of it stands alone. To take one passage or teaching in isolation is like taking one line out of a contract while ignoring the qualifiers on the next page. It will get you in trouble. The whole document makes up the contract.

---

3. Mic. 5:2, 4; Matt. 2:1–8.
4. Hos. 6:6.

In the same way, every page of Scripture makes up the Word of God.[5]

Yet I've noticed that today many of us treat Jesus' words printed in red as if they were more important than the apostles' words printed in black. Like Roman Catholics who stand when the Gospels are read and sit when the Epistles are read, we treat the words of Jesus as if they were far superior to the words of the apostles.

A RICH YOUNG RULER, ZACCHAEUS, AND SOME RICH GUYS IN EPHESUS

The folly of using just a few isolated passages to develop our theology of wealth and of care for the needy can be seen by comparing the significant differences in just three passages: Jesus' command to a rich young ruler, his response to a man named Zacchaeus, and the apostle Paul's instructions to some rich guys in Ephesus. Let's take a look at each one.

The Rich Young Ruler

The story of the rich young ruler is well known. It's one of the favorites for today's money police. It points to the high cost of following Jesus. When the young man was told to sell all he had and give the money to the poor, he couldn't do it. He loved his money too much. It kept him from becoming a disciple.[6]

Most often, this passage is used to challenge us. Are we willing to give it all to Jesus? Are we holding anything back? Are we willing to give up the comforts of the American dream to meet the needs of the poor, or are we saying no to Jesus, just like the rich young ruler did?

People who like to use this story to test our willingness to give up more of what we have to help the poor and needy around the world have missed a few things. To begin with, the issue wasn't the man's wealth. It was his arrogance. He was self-righteous and confident in his own works. He claimed that he'd kept *all* of the com-

---

5. 2 Tim. 3:16–17.
6. Mark 10:17–31; Matt. 19:16–30; Luke 18:18–30.

mandments since his youth. So Jesus asked him to do something he never asked anyone else to do. It went right to the heart of his self-sufficiency. He asked him to take an instant vow of poverty. It's a real stretch to turn this into a passage about our *willingness* to give it all to Jesus. Jesus didn't ask him if he was willing. Jesus told him to sell it all and give the money to the poor. Right now. If we want to apply this passage to everyone, we need to be consistent. We need to insist that we all sell whatever we have and give all the proceeds to the poor and then follow Jesus wherever he takes us.

A Tax Collector Named Zacchaeus

The second story that needs to be included in our theology of money and how God wants us to use it is the story of Zacchaeus. He was a scoundrel, a rich tax collector. And not just any tax collector, a *chief* tax collector. That put him near the top of any sin list. Luke places the story of Zacchaeus in the chapter right after the one about the rich young ruler. That's not an accident. The contrasts between the two are important.

Jesus shocked everybody by inviting himself to Zacchaeus's house. When he arrived, Zacchaeus stood up and promised to give *half* of his *ill-gotten possessions* to the poor and to pay back people he had cheated with a 400 percent return. And Jesus was good with that.

He didn't say, "What about the other half?" He didn't say, "Sorry, it's all or nothing." He said, "Today salvation has come to this house."[7]

Some Rich Guys in Ephesus

The third passage that needs to be included is found in one of the apostle Paul's letters to Timothy. Toward the end of his first letter, he tells him what to say to the rich Christians living in Ephesus. Interestingly, it sounds nothing like Jesus' instruction to the rich young ruler.

Paul tells Timothy to give the rich three instructions: (1) don't be arrogant; (2) don't put your hope in wealth, because it is so

---

7. Luke 19:1–10.

uncertain; and (3) do good, and be rich in good deeds, generous, and willing to share so that you can lay up heavenly treasures.[8]

Not a word about giving it all (or even most of it) to the poor. Not a word about ratcheting down and living more simply. And most surprising of all, he told Timothy to tell the rich that God had provided them with their riches so that they could *enjoy* them as well as share them.[9]

To properly understand God's perspective on wealth and what he wants us to do with the money and the possessions we have, all three of these passages need to be put into the mix along with all the other passages that deal with the subject. We can't claim to speak for God when we're passing on only part of what he's said. Otherwise we're just like the Pharisees, proclaiming a message from God that has more in common with what we wish he said than with what he actually said.

THE POVERTY GOSPEL

Today there's also a strong tendency to read the Bible through the lens of a poverty gospel. This is the predictable pendulum swing away from the nonsense and excesses of the prosperity gospel, which claimed that God wanted everyone healthy and wealthy. The poverty gospel declares the opposite. It asserts that godliness is found in simplicity, suffering, and poverty. It has a built-in bias against wealth.

Try this sometime. Ask a group of younger Christians if the Bible says that money is the root of all evil. Nearly every hand will go up. But that's not what the Bible says. It says that the *love* of money is *a* root of all kinds of evil and that some who were eager to get rich wandered from the faith and brought great grief into their life.[10] The problem isn't money. It's the love of money and an eagerness to get rich that leads to spiritual compromises.

The poverty gospel also assails the American dream. It has no room for a God who blesses us with good things to enjoy. Instead

---

8. 1 Tim. 6:17–19.
9. 1 Tim. 6:17.
10. 1 Tim. 6:9–10.

God wants us to live as simply as possible so that we can give away as much as possible. They won't come right out and say it, but all you have to do is listen to their sermons and read their books, and it becomes clear that today's money police are quite sure that no true disciple would buy a big house, drive an expensive car, go on a fancy vacation, splurge on a nice restaurant, wear designer clothes, or attend a church with elaborate facilities.

I've often wondered what they would have to say to Abraham (or God) about Abraham's great wealth. Surely there were plenty of poor people he could have helped. Same thing with Job. I wonder if some of them would have been numbered among Job's "friends," informing him that his selfish opulence was the reason why God had taken it all away.

Or how about the prayer of a man named Jabez. He asked God to bless him with enlarged borders (make me richer) and to keep him from harm and pain. My money police friends would expect the rest of the verse to say that God struck the selfish twit dead. But that's not what happened. God answered his request and gave him the blessings he asked for.[11]

THE OPULENCE LINE — WHERE IS IT?

I've noticed something else about the gift projections of today's money police. They have an uncanny eye for the line of opulence. They always know where it is in their life and where it is in mine. And to no surprise, the line of what's appropriately simple and generous is always somewhat close to the line they've drawn in their own life.

Is It Opulent to Have More Than We Need?

According to many, if you have more than you need when you're surrounded by a world in need, you're sinfully hoarding. There is no way that God approves of your excess.

Yet that's not what Scripture says. God tells us to be generous. He tells us to help the poor and needy. But he also says that in the household of the wise, you'll find *stores* of *choice* food and oil. That

---

11. 1 Chron. 4:9–10.

sounds like a lot, far more than what they need and a lot better quality than generic brands. He goes on to say that the fool lives on the edge, devouring all he has.[12]

A couple of years ago I heard a proponent of bare-bones living testify to God's provision and blessing in his life. It seems that he'd cut back on his medical insurance to have more money to give away. He saw it as a step of faith and sacrifice we should all consider making. He told how his wife had become sick and nearly died, racking up some huge medical bills that he had no way to pay. But somehow the bills were paid; friends rallied around and paid them off. He used that as proof that God will take care of us if we trust him enough to live day to day and use everything else to take care of the poor.

Apparently, it never dawned on him that the only reason why his bills were paid was that a bunch of his friends had lived wisely enough to store up a margin from which to help him out. They had lived what Scripture calls the life of the wise. He had played the role of a fool and called it faith.

Is It Opulent to Have a Nice House?

The money police also like to bring up the rich fool and his bigger barns. Didn't he pay for those big barns with his life? Well, not exactly. The reason why his life was required of him was not because he had big barns. It was because he was poor toward God. He thought life consisted of his possessions. He was arrogant, trusted in his riches, and failed to generously lay up treasures in heaven. So God said, "You're done." It had nothing to do with the size of his barn. It had everything to do with the size of his heart.[13]

In addition, the early church was surrounded by great poverty, yet there is not one word in the New Testament epistles encouraging the rich to downsize so that they can give more to help out the poor. Perhaps it's because the early church often met in their homes, and people who had estates large enough to have servants

---

12. Prov. 21:20.
13. Luke 12:13–21.

could accommodate more people. They weren't told to simplify; they were told to treat their servants properly, realizing that they too had a master who would someday hold them accountable for how they treated their servants.[14]

Is It Opulent to Waste Money on God?

There's one final story that the money police never seem to bring up. It's the story of a woman in Bethany who extravagantly wasted an alabaster jar of expensive perfume by breaking it and pouring the contents on Jesus' head.[15]

I am sure that if today's money police had been there, they would have been indignant. The perfume would have fetched over a year's wages if sold. It could have gone a long way toward helping the needy. When people harshly rebuked her for her waste, someone said to leave her alone because the poor would always be around for them to help on another day. Talk about a calloused response. Try that line sometime. The money police will go ballistic.

Of course, the person who said, "Leave her alone" and "The poor you will always have with you," was Jesus. He went on to praise her for what she did.

And the people who rebuked her sharply? They were the Pharisees, the religious leaders, and a man named Judas who was so upset that he immediately went to the chief priests to betray Jesus.

That's the problem with becoming self-appointed money police. When we project our gifts and callings on others, we can end up on the wrong side of the Law.

---

14. Eph. 6:9.
15. Mark 14:3–9.

Discussion Questions for Part 7

GIFT PROJECTION

1. What are some of the gifts and callings in your life that you would be most likely to project onto others?

2. From your experience, what are some of the most common gifts and callings that tend to be "gift projected" in your church? To help identify them, think about what typically gets promoted, highlighted, or valued in your church. What gifts, ministries, and callings tend to get ignored?

3. Have you ever been guilty of "gift envy," wishing that you had gifts that others possess and failing to value the gifts God has given to you? If so, where is that most likely to show up? What do you see as the root of these feelings of inferiority or envy?

4. Consider the myth of "full-time ministry."

   a. Do you tend to attribute more dignity and significance to those who serve in professional ministry? If so, why do you think this is so?

b. What could a church do to undercut the myth of full-time ministry and to foster a healthier view of Christian vocation? List as many specific things as you can.

5. Are you prone to be one of the "money police," or are you more likely to be criticized by one?

   a. After reading the chapters in part 7, are there any parts of Scripture that you realize you may have neglected, ignored, or glossed over?

   b. What passages and insights in part 7 did you find to be most challenging or troubling, or that you simply didn't agree with? Why?

A FINAL WORD

Two thousand years ago, some of God's most zealous followers found themselves in a place they never could have imagined. Despite their rigorous study of Scripture and scrupulous obedience of everything they found in it, they'd become the enemies of God. Worse, they were oblivious to what had happened. They actually thought they were his best friends.

I have no doubt that the Pharisees of old had the best of intentions. They wanted to please God and to show others how to please him. I'm sure that they thought their labyrinth of extra rules and spiritual disciplines provided a helpful template for people to follow. And I'm also sure that they considered all of their rules and standards to be solidly biblical. After all, even if none of them were actually found in Scripture, they all were based on Scripture.

They eagerly took it upon themselves to determine who was in and who was out. They thought they were helping God by thinning the herd and keeping the riffraff out. Unfortunately, they had no idea that the people they shooed away were precisely the people God was inviting to the party.

Sadly, the same thing happens today. Well-intentioned Christ followers like you and me can unintentionally sabotage the work of the Lord we claim to serve when we become so focused on what we see as the agenda of God that we lose touch with the heart of God.

We're all susceptible in different ways. The dark side of my zeal may look quite different from yours. But in the end, the pathway to becoming an accidental Pharisee always starts with the same three steps.

1. It begins with a failure to grasp the true gravity and depths of my own sin.
2. It's followed by a heightened disgust for the sins of others.
3. It's then justified by a cut-and-paste theology that emphasizes some of the hard sayings of Jesus while pretty much ignoring those that speak of his compassion, mercy, and grace.

For instance, as we've seen, there are many today who dial in on his instructions to a rich young ruler, telling him to sell everything and give it to the poor in order to follow him and gain eternal life; or his call to deny ourselves, pick up our crosses, die to self, and put our love for him above family, friends, and security; or his warnings that many are called but only few are chosen.

All of these teachings of Jesus are important. They can't be overlooked or ignored. But to understand and apply them properly, they must be interpreted in light of the totality of Scripture and the totality of all that Jesus said and did. Our interpretation of what they mean to us today has to match up with how Jesus actually applied them to the people around him. It has to have room for the same kind of weak, struggling, fearful, and not-yet-ready disciples whom Jesus called to himself, accepted, and put to work in the kingdom.

It has to have room for disciples like Peter, who caved in and vehemently denied Jesus in a moment of weakness. It has to have room for disciples like John Mark, who chickened out and headed home when things proved to be more difficult than expected. And it has to have room for disciples like Joseph of Arimathea, who laid low as a secret disciple out of fear of what it might cost him to go public.

Now, none of these behaviors is commendable. None are excusable. All of them will put us at the back of the following-Jesus line. But here's the good news. None of them automatically disqualify us from being in the line.

While today's modern-day accidental Pharisees want nothing to do with disciples like these, writing them off as disgusting, wimpy, bogus Christians who need to be culled from our churches, Jesus pursued each of them. They were the bruised reeds he would not break and the smoldering wicks he would not snuff out. He put denying Peter to work leading his church. He used chicken John Mark to write one of the gospels, and he chose rich, frightened, secret disciple Joseph to bury his body.

I don't know about you, but that strikes me as incredibly good news. It gives me hope that God really does use crooked sticks to draw straight lines. It gives me hope that grace and mercy aren't merely doctrines to pontificate about.

Now, obviously I'm not saying that we can live like hell and call ourselves disciples. The Bible is quite clear. If we genuinely know God and love him, we will keep his commandments.[1] But I am saying that our definitions of what it means to be a genuine Christ follower must include room for the weak and the struggling, the frightened and the failing, in order to remain aligned with Jesus rather than with the Pharisees of old.

Following Jesus is not a race to see who can be the most radical, sacrificial, knowledgeable, or quickest to burn out. It's not a contest to see who's willing to take the hardest road. That's asceticism, not discipleship.

For the gospel to remain the gospel, grace and mercy have to remain front and center. When the radicalness of my commitment, the intensity of my zeal, or the extent of my personal

---

1. 1 John 2:3–5; John 14:15.

sacrifices become the means to receive or maintain God's acceptance and approval, the good news of the gospel is no longer good news to anyone except those of us who excel.

Make no mistake. My warnings about the dangers of an overzealous faith are not meant as a defense of soft and easy Christianity. They are simply a plea that we remain true to the heart of the gospel, offering rest, help, hope, and salvation to the weary and heavy laden.

None of us live a truly righteous life. Even the best of us—even those at the front of the following-Jesus line—fall far short of the righteousness needed to stand before our God. That's what makes grace so amazing. That's what makes the arrogance of today's accidental Pharisees so sad.

There is nothing praiseworthy in a feel-good, lukewarm, consumer Christianity that never asks us to change or do anything. It makes Jesus gag. But we must never forget that there is also nothing praiseworthy in a spiritual zeal that looks down on others or sublimates Jesus' grace and mercy in order to emphasize our radical obedience and sacrifice. That too makes Jesus gag.

Our hope is not in what we do for God. Our hope is in what God has done for us. That's the gospel. That's discipleship in a nutshell. And that's what keeps people like you and me from becoming accidental Pharisees.

ACKNOWLEDGMENTS

I want to offer a special thanks to those who helped to make this book a reality.

To Chris Brown, Charlie Bradshaw, Paul Savona, the staff, elders board, and congregation of North Coast Church: I owe you all the deepest gratitude for your patience, love, and commitment to the gospel of Jesus Christ. Thank you for encouraging me to serve not only North Coast but also the church at large. You make pastoring a joy.

A special thanks to Erica Brandt for her careful editing and candid feedback. Also, I want to express my gratitude to the entire team at Zondervan, but especially to Ryan Pazdur for his helpful and honest coaching, Andrew Rogers for his tireless efforts to make sure this book gets read, and Brian Phipps and Robin Schmitt for their careful copyediting.

But most of all I want to thank my incredible wife, Nancy: Your careful editing and honest (but kind) feedback made this a much better book. Your fingerprints are on all the good chapters. The not so good ones are all mine. They only serve as proof that I don't always listen as well as I should.

Sticky Church

Larry Osborne

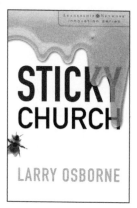

In *Sticky Church*, author and pastor Larry Osborne makes the case that closing the back door of your church is even more important than opening the front door wider. He offers a time-tested strategy for doing so: sermon-based small groups that dig deeper into the weekend message and velcro members to the ministry. It's a strategy that enabled Osborne's congregation to grow from a handful of people to one of the larger churches in the nation—without any marketing or special programming.

Sticky Church tells the inspiring story of North Coast Church's phenomenal growth and offers practical tips for launching your own sermon-based small group ministry. Topics include:

- Why stickiness is so important
- Why most of our discipleship models don't work very well
- Why small groups always make a church more honest and transparent
- What makes groups grow deeper and stickier over time

Sticky Church is an ideal book for church leaders who want to start or retool their small group ministry—and velcro their congregation to the Bible and each other.

Sticky Teams

Keeping Your Leadership Team and Staff on the Same Page

Larry Osborne

Serving as a church leader can be a tough assignment. Whatever your role, odds are you've known your share of the frustration, conflict, and disillusionment that come with silly turf battles, conflicting vision, and marathon meetings.

No doubt, you've asked yourself, "How did it get this way?"

With practical and accessible wisdom, Larry Osborne explains how it got this way. He exposes the hidden roadblocks, structures, and goofy thinking that sabotage even the best intentioned teams. Then with time-tested and proven strategies, he shows what it takes to get (and keep) a board, staff, and congregation on the same page.

Whatever your situation—from start-up, to midsized, to megachurch—Osborne has been there. As the pastor of North Coast Church, he's walked his board, staff, and congregation through the process. Now with warm encouragement and penetrating insights, he shares his secrets to building and maintaining a healthy and unified ministry team that sticks together for the long haul.

Available in stores and online!

NORTH COAST TRAINING NETWORK
Tools & Resources for Pastors

The North Coast Training Network provides consulting, customized workshops, and training events for pastors and ministry teams. For a complete list and schedule, go to www.NorthCoastTraining.org

ADDITIONAL TRAINING RESOURCES BY LARRY OSBORNE
available at www.NorthCoastChurch.com/pastors

SERMON-BASED SMALL GROUP STARTER KIT:

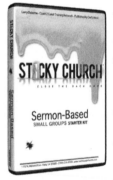

This is a set of DVDs designed to get your sermon-based small group ministry off the ground (or to take your existing groups to new heights). Each of the training sessions is taught by Larry Osborne. The included site license grants you and your church unlimited duplication rights for use within your local church setting.

VIDEO VENUE STARTER KIT:

This is a set of DVDs that features conference and seminar sessions taught by Larry Osborne. It highlights the principles and inner workings behind the successful launch of a Video Venue and is designed for those considering either on-site or multi-site ministry expansion. Each starter kit comes with unlimited duplication rights for use within your local church setting.

Share Your Thoughts

With the Author: Your comments will be forwarded to the author when you send them to *zauthor@zondervan.com*.

With Zondervan: Submit your review of this book by writing to *zreview@zondervan.com*.

Free Online Resources at
www.zondervan.com

Zondervan AuthorTracker: Be notified whenever your favorite authors publish new books, go on tour, or post an update about what's happening in their lives at www.zondervan.com/authortracker.

Daily Bible Verses and Devotions: Enrich your life with daily Bible verses or devotions that help you start every morning focused on God. Visit www.zondervan.com/newsletters.

Free Email Publications: Sign up for newsletters on Christian living, academic resources, church ministry, fiction, children's resources, and more. Visit www.zondervan.com/newsletters.

Zondervan Bible Search: Find and compare Bible passages in a variety of translations at www.zondervanbiblesearch.com.

Other Benefits: Register to receive online benefits like coupons and special offers, or to participate in research.